50 WAYS TO PROTECT YOUR IDENTITY AND YOUR CREDIT

D0827177

50 WAYS TO PROTECT YOUR IDENTITY AND YOUR CREDIT

EVERYTHING YOU NEED TO KNOW
ABOUT IDENTITY THEFT,
CREDIT CARDS, CREDIT REPAIR,
AND CREDIT REPORTS

STEVE WEISMAN

PEARSON
Prentice
Hall

An Imprint of PEARSON EDUCATION
Upper Saddle River, NJ • New York • London • San Francisco • Toronto • Sydney
Tokyo • Singapore • Hong Kong • Cape Town • Madrid
Paris • Milan • Munich • Amsterdam
www.ft-ph.com

SOMERSET CO. LIBRARY
BRIDGEWATER, N.J. 08807

Library of Congress Publication in Data: 2004112968

Vice President and Editor-in-Chief: Tim Moore
Executive Editor: Jim Boyd
Editorial Assistant: Richard Winkler
Development Editor: Russ Hall
Marketing Manager: Martin Litkowski
International Marketing Manager: Tim Galligan
Cover Designer: Chuti Prasertsith
Managing Editor: Gina Kanouse
Senior Project Editor: Lori Lyons
Production: Specialized Composition Inc.
Manufacturing Buyer: Dan Uhrig

©2005 by Pearson Education, Inc.
Publishing as Prentice Hall
Upper Saddle River, New Jersey 07458

Prentice Hall offers excellent discounts on this book when ordered in quantity for bulk purchases or special sales. For more information, please contact U.S. Corporate and Government Sales, 1-800-382-3419, corpsales@pearsontechgroup.com. For sales outside the U.S., please contact International Sales, 1-317-581-3793, international@pearsontechgroup.com.

Company and product names mentioned herein are the trademarks or registered trademarks of their respective owners.

All rights reserved. No part of this book may be reproduced, in any form or by any means, without permission in writing from the publisher.

Printed in the United States of America

First Printing January 2005

10 9 8 7 6 5 4 3

ISBN 0-13-146759-X

Pearson Education LTD.
Pearson Education Australia PTY, Limited.
Pearson Education Singapore, Pte. Ltd.
Pearson Education North Asia, Ltd.
Pearson Education Canada, Ltd.
Pearson Educatión de Mexico, S.A. de C.V.
Pearson Education—Japan
Pearson Education Malaysia, Pte. Ltd.

This book is dedicated to my wife, Carole.

My true identity is found in the love we share.

CONTENTS

ABOUT THE AUTHOR

STEVE WEISMAN hosts the nationally syndicated radio show *A Touch of Grey*, heard on more than 50 stations across America, including New York City's legendary WOR and KRLA Los Angeles. A member of the National Association of Elder Law Attorneys, he has taught at the University of Massachusetts, Curry College, and Boston University, and is an adjunct faculty member at Bentley College. He holds a JD degree from Boston College Law School and is admitted to practice before the United States Supreme Court. Weisman has a legal practice in Cambridge, Massachusetts. He also speaks to groups on legal topics throughout the country. Weisman is legal editor and columnist for *Talkers Magazine*, and writes for publications ranging from *The Boston Globe* to *US Air Magazine*. He has earned a Certificate of Merit from the American Bar Association for excellence in legal journalism. He is the author of *A Guide to Elder Planning: Everything You Need to Know to Protect Yourself Legally & Financially* (Financial Times, Prentice Hall).

INTRODUCTION

dentity theft is one of the most pervasive and insidious crimes of today; a crime that can tremendously disrupt your life—or even put you in jail for crimes you never committed.

This book explains the horrific details of the many identity theft scams that are so prevalent today. Story after story takes you into the dark world of identity theft and the dire consequences that can result from this crime that affects more and more people throughout the world. This book shows you just how vulnerable you are, but it also shows you steps you can take to protect yourself, as best you can, from becoming a victim. It also tells you what to do if you become an identity theft victim.

This book also explains how the world of credit operates and your rights and responsibilities.

Sure, love makes the world go round, but perhaps Joel Grey's character in the musical, *Cabaret* was also right when he said, "Money makes the world go round." Today, however, it is often neither love nor money that sends the world in a spin, but rather credit.

Your credit affects whether you can rent an apartment, buy a home, buy a car, get a job, obtain insurance, or even take a vacation. Your credit is important. And unfortunately, the world of credit is fraught with peril.

You may be discriminated against in credit because of your age, your gender, or your marital status.

The privacy of your financial information may be compromised and widely disseminated to your detriment, making you more vulnerable to identity theft.

Your credit card may have hidden fees, charges, and conditions buried within mountains of "fine print" that can have disastrous effects.

Taking the wrong steps to repair your credit can cause you further financial victimization.

Your credit report, widely used throughout the world of finance and affecting so many areas of your daily life, may be wildly inaccurate or tainted.

This book may scare the hell out of you, and rightfully so. It explains just how vulnerable we all are in the world of identity theft and credit. But it also tells you what you can do about these problems. It provides specific steps you can take to protect your identity and maximize your credit.

1

IDENTITY THEFT

Maybe Shakespeare was right when he said in *Othello*, "Who steals my purse steals trash; 'tis something, nothing; but he that filches from me my good name robs me of that which not enriches him and makes me poor indeed."

Let's say you are at a car dealership and the salesman comes back with a long face and tells you the financing on the car you wanted to buy has been turned down, or the dealership has had to go to another loan source that means higher interest and payments. "But I have great credit," you say.

In another scenario, you apply for another credit card and are turned down. In both cases, you are shown a copy of your credit report and find late payment notices or applications for credit cards in other cities. *Someone has stolen your identity.*

FTC Survey

According to a survey of the Federal Trade Commission[1], 27.3 million Americans were victims of identity theft within a five-year period. Fifty-two percent of identity theft victims first learned that they had been victimized by monitoring their own accounts. Twenty-six percent of victims first learned from credit card issuers, banks, or other companies with which they did business that they had been the victims of identity theft while eight percent of the victims first found out their identity had been stolen when they applied for credit and were turned down. The survey also revealed that most identity thieves use personal information to buy things; however, fifteen percent of all victims were victimized in non-financial ways, such as when an identity thief used the victim's identity when apprehended for another crime by police. Sixty-seven percent of identity theft victims found that their already existing credit card accounts were improperly accessed while nineteen percent of identity theft victims said that their checking or savings accounts had been looted. California was the state with the highest number of identity theft victims proportionate to its population, followed by Arizona, Nevada, Texas, Florida, New York, Washington, Maryland, Oregon, and Colorado. The states with the lowest frequency of identity theft in proportion to population and in descending order were Wyoming, Montana, Maine, Kentucky West Virginia, Iowa, Vermont, South Dakota, and North Dakota. North Dakota had only 12.6 victims of identity theft for every 100,000 of population during 2002.

The FTC has been helping identity theft victims since 1998 and has an excellent Identity Theft Program to help victims and provide information to help combat this problem. If you are the victim of identity theft you can file a complaint with the FTC by calling them at 1-877-IDTHEFT or online at www.consumer.gov/idtheft. When a complaint is made, the information is stored and made available to law enforcement agencies around the country. Victims should not be concerned that the information will make them susceptible to further identity theft; the database is safe and secure.

A Big Problem

Frank Abagnale is a former identity thief who has left, as they say in *Star Wars*, the dark side of the force and is now a recognized expert on personal security matters. His exploits were described in his book, *Catch Me If You Can*, which was later made into a hit movie starring Leonardo DiCaprio and Tom Hanks.

In an interview with bankrate.com he spoke about one of the major problems in fighting identity theft: "Visa and MasterCard have losses amounting to $1.3 billion a year from stolen, forged, altered cards or those applied for under false pretenses. In the end they will probably raise fees and service charges to recoup these losses."

Abagnale went on to say, "Banks and corporations have found it is easier to write off a loss than it is to prosecute it. Most district attorneys have a benchmark set and do not prosecute forged checks under $5,000. Most U.S. attorneys have a benchmark of $250,000 before prosecuting white-collar crimes, and the

TITLE: 50 ways to protect your identity
BARCODE: 33665017643470
DUE DATE: 11-22-17

TITLE: The Black Hand : the epic war bet
BARCODE: 33665030843446
DUE DATE: 11-22-17

TITLE: The Lufthansa heist : behind the
BARCODE: 33665028626571
DUE DATE: 11-22-17

TITLE: Skyjack : the hunt for D.B. Coope
BARCODE: 33665024404908
DUE DATE: 11-22-17

TITLE: Cemetery John : the undiscovered
BARCODE: 33665026866070
DUE DATE: 11-22-17

FBI is under a directive not to investigate crimes under $100,000. The problem for the government agencies and municipalities is the lack of manpower and resources to prosecute these crimes."

Treasury Secretary John W. Snow on Identity Theft

In a speech in June of 2003 Treasury Secretary John W. Snow said, "The wretched depravity of some identity crimes defies the imagination. In a ring stretching from New Jersey to California, a healthcare worker in cahoots with bank insiders and mortgage brokers got the names of terminally ill hospital patients, forged their identities, drained their bank accounts, and then bought houses and cars in their names—stealing their identity and looting their finances. Another recent case involved a rash of scammers posing in military uniforms who visited the wives of soldiers deployed in Iraq. They falsely informed the wives that their husbands had been seriously wounded. The con artists then tried to collect personal information about the soldiers from the distraught wives, to enable the scammers to use the soldiers' identities and steal the families' savings."

Terrorism and Identity Theft

Although the connection between terrorism and identity theft might not be immediately apparent, it is very real and threatening.

In his testimony of September 9, 2003, before the Senate Committee on Finance regarding the homeland security and terrorism threat from document fraud, identity theft, and Social Security number misuse, FBI acting Assistant Director of the Counterterrorism Division, John S. Pitole said, "Advances in computer hardware and software along with the growth of the Internet has significantly increased the role that identity theft plays in crime. For example, the skill and time needed to produce high-quality counterfeit documents has been reduced to the point that nearly anyone can be an expert. Criminals and terrorists are now using the same multimedia software used by professional graphic artists. Today's software allows novices to easily manipulate images and fonts, allowing them to produce high-quality counterfeit documents. The tremendous growth of the Internet, the accessibility it provides to such an immense audience coupled with the anonymity it allows result in otherwise traditional fraud schemes becoming magnified when the Internet is utilized as part of the scheme. This is particularly true with identity theft related crimes. Computer intrusions into the databases of credit card companies, financial institutions, online businesses, etc. to obtain credit card or other identification information for individuals have launched countless identity theft related crimes."

"The methods used to finance terrorism range from the highly sophisticated to the most basic. There is virtually no financing method that has not at some level been exploited by these groups. Identity theft is a key catalyst fueling many of these methods. For example, an Al-Qaeda terrorist cell in Spain used stolen credit cards in fictitious sales scams and for numerous other purchases for the cell. They kept purchases below amounts where identification would be presented. They also used stolen telephone and credit cards for communications back to Pakistan, Afghanistan, Lebanon, etc. Extensive use of false passports and travel documents were used to open bank accounts where money for the Mujahadin movement was sent to and from countries such as Pakistan, Afghanistan, etc."

Patriot Act

A particularly insidious identity theft scam uses the Patriot Act as a ruse to get your personal financial information. Again, it starts with an e-mail, this time purporting to be from the Federal Deposit Insurance Corporation (FDIC) that says that Department of Homeland Security Director Tom Ridge has notified the FDIC to suspend all deposit insurance on your bank accounts due to possible violations of the Patriot Act. After luring you into the trap, the criminal sending the e-mail then tells you within the e-mail that all your FDIC insurance will be suspended until you provide verification of personal financial information, such as your bank account numbers.

Warning   *The FDIC does not send out e-mails for these purposes. Never provide personal financial information over the Internet unless you have initiated the contact and you are absolutely sure of with whom you are dealing.*

What Do Identity Thieves Do?

Identity thieves take your personal information and use it to harm you in a number of ways including:

- Gaining access to your credit card account, bank account, or brokerage account.

- Opening new credit card accounts in your name.

- Opening new bank accounts in your name.

- Buying cars and taking out car loans in your name.

- Buying cell phones in your name.

- Using your name when committing crimes.

Although you may not be responsible for fraudulent charges, the damage to your credit as reflected in your credit report can affect your employment, insurance applications, and loan applications as well as any future credit arrangements you may wish to establish.

❧ Nowhere Are You Safe

In November of 2003, in Virginia, an emergency medical technician was arrested and charged with credit card theft, credit card fraud, attempted grand larceny, and identity theft stemming from an incident that occurred when the EMT was called to a nursing home to assist an eighty-year-old resident. While going through her purse for identification, he took one of her credit cards. When he returned to the fire station, he went online using the fire department's computer to order a 42-inch plasma televi sion paid for by the stolen credit card. Fortunately, the credit card company was vigilant and flagged this unusual purchase for an elderly nursing home resident. They called the victim's daughter who managed her mother's financial affairs. She promptly told the credit card company that it was a mistake. It did not take Sherlock Holmes to identify the villain because the stupid thief gave the address of the fire station as the delivery address for the television. Due to prompt action in investigating the matter, the television never was delivered. The computer provided further information that led to identifying the EMT who had helped himself to his victim's identity.

❧ Dumpster Diving

Dumpster diving is the name for the practice of going through trash for "goodies" such as credit card applications and other items considered to be junk by the person throwing out the material. In the hands of an identity thief, some of this trash can be transformed into gold. Go to any post office and inevitably you will find in their trash containers much of this material that owners of post office boxes toss out when they go through their mail before they even leave the post office. Too often people do not even bother to tear up the items. In the case of pre-approved credit card offers, all the identity thief has to do is fill in the application, change the address, and send it back to the bank. In short order the thief will receive a credit card and a careless individual will become the victim of identity theft as the identity thief begins to use the credit card and runs up debts in the victim's name.

❧ The Drug Connection

Steven Massey was convicted of conspiracy to commit computer fraud and mail theft for his operation of an identity theft ring in which he enlisted methamphetamine addicts to plunder mail-boxes and a recycling center for pre-approved credit card applications and other material that could be utilized for identity theft. Methamphetamine addicts are perfectly suited for identity theft. They often stay awake for days at a time and can patiently perform boring tasks such as going through mail and even piecing together torn credit card solicitations. Drug money for identity theft information is a growing problem throughout the country. This match between identity theft and methamphetamine addicts was even a topic of discussion in Congressional hearings in 2003.

Phishing—Go Phish

You may remember the commercials by Citibank about its identity theft protections in which the voice of a young woman describing the bustier she bought with her credit card comes out of the body of an overweight, slovenly man. The ads made their point, but unfortunately so did the identity thieves who targeted Citibank and other companies through a tactic known as "phishing" in which they sent e-mails to unsuspecting consumers telling them that they needed to click on a hyperlink to update their information with the companies. When unsuspecting victims clicked on the hyperlink, they came to a website that looked like the real McCoy, or Citibank for that matter, but it was a phony. When the consumer entered his or her personal information, such as Social Security number or a credit card number, the identity thief had all he or she needed to either use the information to steal the identity of the victim or sell the information to other thieves. In the last two months of 2003, Citibank issued fourteen alerts to its customers warning them of this dangerous scam.

The term "phishing" goes back to the early days of America Online (AOL) when it charged its customers an hourly rate. Young Internet users with an addiction to their computers, not very much cash, and bit of larceny in their hearts sent e- mails or instant messages through which they purported to be AOL customer service agents. In these phony e-mails under those false pretenses they would ask for the unwary victim's passwords in order to stay online on someone else's dime. After a while, this phony fishing expedition for information came to be known as "phishing."

Phishing with a Pal

PayPal is a company with which anyone who has ever bought something on eBay is familiar. PayPal is an online payment service, owned by eBay, used to securely transfer money electronically. Through the popularity of eBay's online auction site, PayPal has gathered forty million customers who use its services to make sure that the exchange of funds for auctioned items is done safely and securely. But for many people that safety and security are an illusion. Through phishing, a con man sets up a website that imitates a legitimate website, such as PayPal, but whose sole purpose is to obtain sensitive personal financial information that can be used to facilitate identity theft. With the computer and software technology so readily available to pull off such a crime, the skill and artistry of the forgers of yesterday are not needed by the identity stealing phishers of today.

Through phony e-mails that looked like they were from PayPal, the identity thieves contacted retailers that used PayPal's services and requested confirmation of their passwords and other account information. According to PayPal, the passwords requested provided the criminals with access to sales information, but fortunately the personal financial information of their customers is stored on separate secure computer servers that are inaccessible to merchants or others that use PayPal's services. That is the good news. The bad news is that, armed with customers' names and other information about their previous purchases obtained through this scam, the con men were in a position to contact the customers directly and trick the unwary customers into revealing personal financial information that opened the door to identity theft. In the past, con men have sent e-mails purporting to be from PayPal, telling the customers that their accounts would be put on a restricted status until they completed a credit card confirmation that could be found on the PayPal site to which the e-mail directed the consumer. Unfortunately, the Web site to which the consumers were directed was a phony site used by the criminals to phish for victims. Previously, criminals would just randomly send out millions of e-mail messages, hoping to snag a few unwary victims. However, armed with personal account information surreptitiously obtained from PayPal using merchants, the phony e-mails would appear more legitimate and thus they were more likely to take in more victims.

Warning   *PayPal never asks for personal financial information by way of e-mail and never refers to previous transactions through e-mail. If you get such an e-mail, do not reply to it, but inform PayPal by telephone directly of the e-mail message you received.*

Former Good Advice
Smug consumers used to be able to identify a phishing expedition by merely looking at the Web browser's address window to determine whether the e-mail purporting to be from some company with which they generally deal

was legitimate. If the sender's e-mail address began with an unusual number configuration or had random letters, it indicated that it was phony. The e-mail addresses of legitimate companies are usually simple and direct. Unfortunately, this is no longer the case. Now computer savvy identity thieves are able to mimic the legitimate e-mail addresses of legitimate companies.

Two Things to Look For

When identity thieves mimic a legitimate company's e-mail address using the latest technology, there will be no SSL padlock icon in the lower corner of your browser. SSL is the abbreviation for Secure Sockets Layer, an Internet term for a protocol for transmitting documents over the Internet in an encrypted and secure fashion. In addition, when you type a different URL (the abbreviation for Uniform Resource Locator, the address of material found on the World Wide Web) into what appears to be the address bar, the browser's title will not change from the phony "welcome message."

More Good Advice

Don't fall for the bait. It takes a few moments longer, but if you are in any way inclined to respond to an e-mail that could be phishing to send you to a phony website, do not click on the hyperlink in the e-mail that purports to send you to the company's website. Rather, type in what you know to be the proper website address for the company with which you are dealing.

AOL Scam

In a phishing case brought by the FTC and the Justice Department, it was alleged that Zachary Keith Hill sent out e-mails to consumers that looked like they were from America Online. The e-mail address of the sender indicated it was from the billing center or account department, and the subject line contained a warning such as "AOL Billing Error Please Read Enclosed Email" or "Please Update Account Information Urgent." The e-mail itself warned the victim that if he or she did not respond to the e-mail, his or her account would be cancelled. The e-mail also contained a hyperlink to send unwary consumers to a web page that looked like an AOL Billing Center. But it was a phony web page operated by Hill. At the web page, the victim was prompted to provide information such as Social Security number, bank account numbers and bank routing numbers as well as other information. Hill, in turn, used this information to facilitate identity theft. The FTC eventually settled its charges against Hill, who agreed to refrain from ever sending e-mail spam or setting up fictitious and misleading websites. As with just about all FTC settlements, Hill did not admit to violating the law, but he did promise not to do it again.

Phishing with a Large Net

The Phishing Attack Trends Report is published monthly online at www.antiphishing.org by the Anti-Phishing Working Group, an organization dedicated to eliminating identity theft resulting from phishing. In a recent monthly report the report stated that the companies most often imitated by phony phishing websites were eBay, Citibank, AOL, and PayPal.

Phishing Around the World

In an effort to clean up its own house, EarthLink, the Internet access provider, went on a phishing expedition, trying to trace the purveyors of phony phishing schemes, and what they found was both startling and disturbing. Many of the phishing scams they were able to track originated in e-mails from around the world, particularly Russia, Romania, other Eastern European countries, and Asia. In Romania, Dan Maarius Stefan was convicted of stealing almost a half a million dollars through a phishing scam and sentenced to 30 months in prison

For every computer geek or small time phisher, such as convicted identity thief Helen Carr who used phony e-mail messages purporting to be from AOL to steal people's money, it appears that more sophisticated organized crime phishing rings are popping up, posing a serious threat to computer users. This presents a growing problem for law enforcement.

> ## ❧ National Do Not E-Mail Registry
>
> The National Do Not Call Registry administered by the Federal Trade Commission has been a boon to many people who do not wish to be annoyed by telemarketers. It would only seem logical that a national do not e-mail list would offer similar benefits to people wishing to avoid spam, the commonly used term for junk e-mail. It might seem logical, but there is no law providing for such a list. When you see a solicitation to sign up for a "National Do Not E-Mail Registry" what you are actually seeing is another phishing expedition seeking to snare your personal information and steal your identity. Don't fall for it.

How Do You Know That You Have Been a Victim of Phishing?

The problem is that you may not know that you have been a victim of identity theft through phishing. When a mugger takes your wallet, you know right away that your money has been taken, but when an identity thief steals your identity through phishing, you may not remember what appeared to be the innocuous e-mail that started you on the road to having your identity stolen. As always, an ounce of prevention is worth a gigabyte of cure.

What You Can Do to Prevent Identity Theft

1. Do a little spring-cleaning in your wallet or purse even if it is the middle of the summer. Do you really need to carry all the cards and identifications that you presently carry?

2. If you rent a car while on vacation, remember to destroy your copy of the rental agreement after you have returned the car. Don't leave it in the glove compartment.

3. Stolen mail is a ripe source of identity theft. When you are traveling, you may want to have a neighbor you trust pick up your mail every day or have your mail held at the post office until your return. Extremely careful people or extremely paranoid people, depending on your characterization of the same people, may prefer to use a post office box rather than a mailbox at home. Identity thieves also get your mail by filling out a "change of address" form using your name to divert your mail to them. If you find you are not receiving any mail for a couple of days, it is worth contacting your local postmaster to make sure everything is okay. A recent preventive measure instituted by the U.S. Postal Service requires post offices to send a "Move Validation Letter" to both the old and the new address whenever a change of address is filed. If you receive one of these notices and you have not changed your address, you should respond immediately because it could well be a warning that an identity thief has targeted you. A careful credit card holder keeps an eye on his or her mailbox for the arrival each month of his or her monthly statement from the credit card company. If a bill is missing, it may mean that someone has hijacked your account and filed a change of address form with the credit card issuer to buy some more time. The sooner you become aware that security of your account has been compromised, the better off you will be. You should also be particularly watchful of the mail when your card is close to expiration. An identity thief may be in a position to steal your mail containing your new card. If an identity thief is armed with enough personal information to activate the card, you could be in trouble.

4. Prudent people may wish to use travelers' checks while on vacation rather than taking their checkbook because an enterprising identity thief who manages to get your checkbook can access your checking account and drain it.

5. Be wary of who may be around you when you use an ATM machine. Someone may be looking over your shoulder at you inputting your PIN number. That same someone may lift your wallet shortly thereafter. Next step—disaster.

6. Make copies of all your credit cards front and back so that you can tell whether a card has been lost or stolen. Also keep a list of the customer

service telephone numbers for each card. When copying your cards, you may wish to consider whether you really need that many cards.

7. Be careful storing personal information and mail even in your own home. In April of 2004, Shreveport, Louisiana, police arrested a babysitter on identity theft charges. They alleged that she stole a credit application mailed to the people for whom she was babysitting and also opened other accounts using the Social Security number of her employer that she had found while rummaging through their documents.

8. After you have received a loan, a credit card, or anything else that required you to complete an application containing your Social Security number, request that your Social Security number be removed from the application kept on record. In addition, if you are feeling particularly paranoid, ask that your credit report used by the bank or other institution be shredded in your presence. They no longer need that information after you have received the loan.

9. Make life easier for yourself. Remove yourself from the marketing lists for pre-approved credit cards and other solicitations. You can remove yourself from the Direct Marketing Association's solicitation list by writing to them at Mail Preference Service, Direct Marketing Association, P.O. Box 9008, Farmingdale, NY 11735. Include your name and address, but no other personal information. You can also register for the Direct Marketing Association's Mail Preference Service to opt out of national mailing lists online at www.dmaconsumers.org, but there is a five-dollar charge for doing so. DMA members are required to remove people who have registered with the Mail Preference Service from their mailings. However, because the list is distributed only four times a year, it may take about three months from the time that your name has been entered to see a reduction in junk mail.

10. Register with the Direct Marketing Association's E-Mail Preference Service to opt out of national e-mail lists. Again, although this will reduce your spam e-mail, it will not eliminate it because many spammers are not members of the Direct Marketing Association. You can register for the E-mail Preference Service online at www.dmaconsumers.org/consumers/optoutform.

11. If you do get unwanted spam e-mails, do not click on the "remove me" link provided by many spam e-mails. All you will succeed in doing is letting them know that you are an active address and you will end up receiving even more unwanted e-mails.

12. If you receive spam faxes, you also should be wary of contacting the telephone number to remove yourself from their lists. It is already illegal for you to have received the spam fax. Contacting the sender by its telephone removal number may cost you for the call and will not reduce your spam faxes.

13. Sign up for the National Do Not Call Registry to reduce unwanted telemarketing calls. Most telemarketers are legitimate. Almost all are annoying, and many are criminals setting you up for identity theft. In order to sign up for the Do Not Call Registry, you may call toll free 1-888-382-1222 or register online at www.donotcall.gov.

14. Check your credit report at least annually and remember to get copies from each of the three major credit report bureaus, all of which independently compile the information contained in their files. Look over your file and make sure everything is in order. Particularly look for unauthorized and inaccurate charges or accounts. Also, check out the section of your report that deals with inquiries. A large number of inquiries that you have not authorized could be the tracks of an identity thief trying to open accounts in your name. A large number of inquiries can also have the harmful effect of lowering your credit score.

15. Check your annual Social Security statement as provided by the Social Security Administration annually. It provides an estimate of your Social Security benefits and your contributions and can be helpful in detecting fraud. It is also a good thing to check this statement carefully each year to make sure that the information contained within it is accurate to insure that you are slated to receive all the Social Security benefits to which you are entitled.

Endnotes

1. Released in September of 2003.

2

MAKING YOURSELF LESS VULNERABLE TO IDENTITY THEFT

Identity thieves believe that they deserve a lot of credit. Unfortunately, the credit to which they are convinced they are entitled is yours. Credit cards present an all too easy target for identity thieves. Protecting your credit cards from identity theft should be a priority for everyone. Take the following steps to reduce your chances of being the victim of credit card fraud:

1. Sign your credit card as soon as you receive it and activate it. Some people believe that instead of signing your credit card you should write "See ID" on the signature line on the back of the card. The hope is that whenever your card is used, the clerk or whoever is processing your purchase will check your ID to make sure that it is you that is using your credit card. It sounds like a good idea, but credit card issuers are in general agreement that it is best to sign your card. Under the rules enforced between merchants and the major credit card issuers, such as Visa, MasterCard and American Express, a merchant is supposed to compare the signature on the sales slip with the signature on the credit card. The merchant should refuse to go through with the transaction if the cardholder refuses to sign his or her card.

2. As much as possible, do not let your credit card out of your sight when you make a purchase; a significant amount of credit card fraud occurs when the salesperson with whom you are dealing, out of your view, swipes your card through a small apparatus that gathers all of the information imbedded in your card. The thief then uses that information to make charges to your account.

3. Save your receipts and ultimately destroy those receipts by shredding.

4. Never give credit card information over the phone to anyone unless you have initiated the call.

✒ Online Shopping Credit Card Protection

The opportunities for identity theft during online shopping are magnified. Two ways of reducing the odds are through the use of either a single-use card number provided to you by your card issuer or by the establishment of a password to be used when your credit card is used online.

The single-use authorization number is tied to your credit card, but has a distinct one-time effectiveness so that even if the number is compromised, your credit remains safe from identity theft.

Even less bothersome to a regular online shopper is the use of a password that you set up with your credit card issuer. When you enter your credit card number during an online purchase, a pop-up box will appear requesting your password. After you enter the password, the transaction continues. As further security, the internet retailer with which you are dealing never sees or has access to your password. So, even if the retailer's security is breached, your credit card is safe.

Lottery Scams

Let's face it. Winning a lottery is difficult enough, but it certainly is made more difficult if you have not even entered, which is why when you are notified that you have won a lottery that you did not enter, you should be skeptical. You should be even more skeptical if the e-mail message informing you of your good fortune asks for some personal information from you such as a bank account number. It's a scam, and its sole purpose is to make you the victim of identity theft.

Vote for Me

Identity thieves are both inventive and knowledgeable of the times. During a recent period when many political organizations were busy encouraging and assisting people in registering to vote, identity thieves were also being heard from. In Midway, Florida, identity thieves posing as members of legitimate political organizations went door to door pretending to assist residents in registering to vote, but were actually gathering personal information such as Social Security numbers to use for identity theft.

❧ Stories and Warnings: Enterprising Inmates

Although it certainly does not qualify as rehabilitation, the conviction in 2003 of James Sabatino of wire fraud does show that some prison inmates are doing more with their time than just sitting around watching television. James Sabatino was serving a twenty-seven month sentence for threatening federal prosecutors when he managed to steal the identities of a number of prominent business executives and use the information gathered through these identity thefts to purchase close to a million dollars worth of goods and services, all the while serving his prison sentence. It takes time to steal that much stuff, and Sabatino spent about eight hours a day on the phone committing his crimes. During the course of one month alone, Sabatino placed a thousand telephone calls from his cell (I expect he used a cell phone—all puns intended). In fact, Sabatino used his cell phone to order more cell phones from Nextel using the identity of a Sony Pictures Entertainment executive. The phones were sent to a phony Sony address (try saying that out loud) that in actuality was a Federal Express office where an accomplice retrieved the phones. Sabatino's ultimate undoing began when an alert executive at Sony, Jack Kindberg, received invoices for the purchase of thirty cell phones he had never ordered. Corporate security eventually traced the thievery to James Sabatino, who pleaded guilty to wire fraud and was sentenced to more than eleven years in prison. Maybe Sony Pictures will make a movie out of his story.

Do Not Call

You may be like me and were thrilled to sign up for the national do-not-call registry to make your telephone off limits to telemarketers. However, as an example of how everything is an opportunity for con men, a recent scam involves your being called by someone purporting to be from either your state's do-not-call list or the National Do Not Call List who asks you to verify some personal information for the list. Again, there is no reason why anyone operating a do-not-call list needs any information other than your telephone number. Remember Steve's Rule number one—never give out personal information to anyone over the phone whom you have not called and always be sure of to whom you are speaking.

Cell Phone Cameras

Even if you do not have one of the new cell phones that takes photographs, we have all seen the clever advertising used by the telephone companies to convince us that we just cannot live a tolerable existence without one of these new phones. But as with many advances in technology, there is concern that criminals will use this advance to assist in identity theft. The concern is that someone utilizing a cell phone with a camera incorporated into it will photograph your credit card or your PIN number and then use the information gained to steal your identity. The reality is that despite the advertisements that make them look so good, the quality of the photograph that you get from your cell phone is not sufficient to provide the kind of detail you need to read a credit card. But as technology improves, the opportunities for identity theft will increase as well. So be a little more careful ahead of the curve.

A Danger in the Workplace

According to the research of Professor Judith Collins of Michigan State University, approximately 70% of all identity theft can be traced back to employees stealing personal information. As recently as April 25, 2002, the Office of the Comptroller of the Currency, a part of the United States Treasury Department, sent a warning to all national banks in which it alerted banks to the activities of organized gangs of criminals who infiltrated banks through their tellers in order to perform identity theft and other crimes.

≈ Inside Job

In February of 2004, Thoung Mong Nguyen was sentenced to 12 years in prison and ordered to repay 1.3 million dollars for operating an identity theft ring in which stolen credit card numbers and phony IDs were used to make purchases charged to their victims. A rogue employee of the Bank of America provided Nguyen with personal information such as Social Security numbers belonging to customers of the bank. This information was used to obtain driver's licenses and credit cards that were used by the criminals for fraudulent purchases.

Identity Theft and the ATM

If an identity thief uses your ATM card or debit card, the federal Electronic Fund Transfer Act provides you with some protection. The amount of your protection, however is significantly affected by how fast you notify the bank that you have been victimized. The maximum amount for which you may be held responsible for a stolen ATM card is $50 if you notify the bank within two business days of learning that your card has been lost or stolen. If you delay notifying your bank more than two business days after discovering that your card has been lost or been used improperly, but within 60 days of receiving a statement showing that the card has been used for an unauthorized transaction, the maximum amount of your personal financial responsibility for the misuse of the card is $500. But if you wait more than 60 days after learning of the unauthorized use, you stand to lose everything that was taken from your account between the end of the sixty-day period and the time that you reported your card was missing. It is best to notify your bank by telephone first and then immediately follow up your call with a written notification. A sample notification letter can be found in Chapter 15, "Forms." It is important to note that, regardless of the law, both Visa and MasterCard have taken the consumer-friendly action of limiting their customers' liability for unauthorized debit card use to $50, regardless of the time it takes the customer to notify the bank.

A Primer on ATM Identity Theft

As bank robber Willie Sutton said, he robbed banks because that is where the money is. That also explains the attraction to identity thieves of Automatic Teller Machines (ATMs). ATMs offer an easy way to use identity theft to steal people's money. The plain, hard fact is that ATMs are vulnerable. There are a number of ways to steal money through an ATM.

Not all ATMs are owned by banks. Private individuals, who are able to earn significant fees for ATM use by their customers, own many ATMs. To set up a private ATM business, one needs an ATM, sufficient money to stock the machine, and a bank account into which the ATM card user's bank can send the funds necessary to reimburse the ATM owning businessman for the money withdrawn and the use fee. There are no government regulations or licensing requirements. The banking industry itself sponsors independent service organizations that control the connecting of the privately owned machines to the bank networks. These independent service organizations, or ISOs, are intended to investigate and approve new private ATM owners, but the oversight is not particularly strong.

The owner of a privately owned ATM can install a mechanism within the machine that takes down and stores the account numbers and Personal Identification Numbers (PINs) of the people using the machine. The ATM-owning identity thief then just harvests the names, account numbers, and PINs and uses that information to steal money from the bank accounts of unwary victims.

Another scheme involves tampering with legitimate bank owned and operated ATMs by installing a thin, phony keypad over the real keypad. This phony keypad records PIN numbers and enables identity thieves to obtain sensitive, personal information without ever having to get at the inner workings of the ATM. The thieves just go back and retrieve their phony keypad whenever they think they have captured enough victims and download the information. Then they are off to the races.

A third way that people have their identities stolen at ATMs is through the use of small, hidden cameras that look over the shoulders of customers inputting their PINs. The cameras record the PINs and the identity thieves watch the whole transaction without having to be anywhere near the ATM.

What Can You Do to Protect Yourself from Identity Theft at the ATM?

1. Avoid privately owned ATMs. Whenever possible, use ATM machines of your own bank. This not only saves you from an increased danger of identity thievery, it also will lower the fees you would otherwise pay for merely accessing your own bank account.

2. Take a careful look at any ATM you are using for indications that its exterior has been tampered with.

3. Look around for hidden cameras. Banks themselves will have cameras, but they are generally imbedded in the ATM itself.

The Race to Catch an ATM Identity Thief

Due to the daily limits on the maximum amount of money that you can take out of your bank account through an ATM, large-scale rings of identity thieves have to spend a significant amount of time feeding their phony cards, which carry the stolen information, into legitimate ATMs. One New York City ring was busted in 2001 following the complaints of customers who had noticed that their accounts had been raided. Armed with the numbers of the hijacked accounts and a software program that could locate the specific ATM at which a card was being used, law enforcement was ready for the chase. And a chase it was. Rushing to locations in a crowded city like New York City is no simple task. At times, Secret Service agents stuck in traffic literally had to jump out of their cars and run to the ATM locations in order to try and arrive in time to catch their quarry red handed. But just as con man Professor Harold Hill said early in the play, *The Music Man* you have to know the territory. And these identity thieves knew the territory. They changed their method of operation to make their ATM withdrawals during the busiest times of the day when both the New York City streets and the sidewalks would be the most congested. And rather than take the time to use card after compromised card at individual ATMs, the identity thieves kept on the move, using fewer cards at as many as 500 ATM machines. In order to counter the latest chess moves by the identity thieves, law enforcement began to stake out ATMs that had been the sites of previous fraudulent withdrawals. Then a break finally came. On November 15, 2001, a Citibank employee using ATM withdrawal software noticed that $7,000 had just been withdrawn from a number of different accounts in quick succession at the same ATM. The Secret Service was promptly notified and rushed to the ATM. After a short chase, an arrest was made and the ring was broken.

Identity Theft and Young People

Although it only presently accounts for about 2% of the identity theft in America today, an FTC study showed identity theft from people under the age of 18 could be significant. It can be particularly problematic for a child to have his or her identity stolen because it may not be discovered until many years after the crime. Young people going to college may find when they apply for financial aid that an identity thief has seriously compromised their credit.

Unfortunately, a growing trend in identity theft is the victimization of children by their own parents who are in a unique position to financially abuse their children by establishing credit in the names of their children. Parents apply for Social Security numbers in the names of their minor children, and if mail comes that would indicate that something out of the ordinary has occurred, such as a credit card statement for a nine-year-old child, the parent is in a position to intercept the mail.

Mailboxes and Identity Theft

Most mailboxes come equipped with small red flags that when raised indicate the owner of the mailbox has outgoing mail to be picked up by the mailman. They also can serve as an invitation to identity thieves to raid your mail. An old fashioned, but still viable, form of stolen mail identity theft occurs when your mail, containing checks to creditors such as credit card companies or your mortgage payment, is grabbed by an identity thief. The thief performs a process known as "check washing" through which the amount of the check and the name of the payee is changed from the person or business to which you made out the check to the name of the identity thief. Common household cleaning products such as bleach can be used to "wash" the check and remove the name of the payee. The check is then rewritten payable to the identity thief in an amount of the thief's choosing.

It is not just your outgoing mail that is fodder for identity thieves. Mail left in your mailbox by the mailman can include new credit cards, Social Security checks, income tax refunds, credit card applications and credit card statements as well as other documents that can be utilized for identity theft purposes.

Not even legitimate United States Postal Service mailboxes are safe from identity thieves. In April 2004, law enforcement investigators uncovered an identity theft ring in Indiana that utilized a combination of high technology computers with a low technology metal device that the identity thieves installed in the familiar United States Postal Service blue mailboxes found on many street corners and into which we all deposit our mail. The device that resembles a snorkel is called a "mail stop." It collects the mail that later was gathered by the mail thieves without having to make an apparent break into the mailbox which would have alerted postal authorities. What the thieves looked for was the usual sensitive material, checks and billing account information that could be transformed through sophisticated computer programs to produce phony driver's licenses and blank checks.

Tip   *When mailing checks, mail them directly from the post office. Or better yet, try secure online bill paying. As for incoming mail, you may consider a locked mailbox or a post office box at the post office.*

More Tips for Making Yourself Safer from Identity Theft

The bad news is that you can't do anything to guarantee that you will not become the victim of identity theft. The good news is that there are a number of simple (and not so simple) steps that you can take that can reduce your chances of becoming an identity theft victim. Some seem a bit excessive, and perhaps they are, but the decision is up to you. Remember, even paranoids have enemies.

1. Consider paying bills online. It can be cheaper and more secure. But be sure that the online service you are using has security protection. Anytime you provide personal information online, make sure that the site is secure. On Internet Explorer, look for the little lock symbol that shows your information is being encrypted.

2. Check your bank statements, telephone statements, credit card statements and brokerage account statements for unauthorized charges. Each month when you get your statements, scrutinize them carefully to make sure that every charge is legitimate. Keep your statements in a safe and secure place. Shred the statements when you no longer need them. If a monthly bill does not arrive on time, promptly notify the company. Sometimes a thief will use your personal information to get your credit card company or other company with which you do business to send your bill to a new address. In this way, the identity thief is able to prolong the period that he or she is able to fraudulently use your account before you or the company becomes aware of its improper use.

3. Your mother was right. Don't talk to strangers. Updating Mom's advice, don't talk to strangers online. Do not download files to you from people you do not know. Not only could your computer be damaged through a virus; it also could subject you to computer programs commonly called "spyware" that permit an identity thief to access your personal information.

4. Do not carry your Social Security card in your wallet.

5. Get a shredder to destroy all your unnecessary financial records as well as pre-approved credit card offers. Dumpster diving identity thieves can go through your trash to find the mother load of information for identity theft.

6. Do not write down your PIN number or passwords. However, be sure whatever PIN or password you choose is not something that is easily associated with you, such as your name or your pet's name.

7. Do not store your personal information on your laptop computer. Laptop computers present a tantalizing target for thieves. Many people prepare their income tax returns on their computers, forgetting about the sensitive personal financial information that may be left on their hard drives. Always remove this information from your computer upon completion of your tax return.

8. Get a good anti-virus software program and keep it constantly updated. Viruses can infect your computer with spyware programs that, unbeknownst to you, may cause your computer to send information stored on your computer to the hacker that can facilitate identity theft.

9. Set up a firewall on your computer. A firewall is a computer program that makes it more difficult for hackers to get access to your computer by preventing or selectively blocking access to your computer through the internet There are many good firewall programs that are easy to install on your computer

10. When you get rid of your computer it is not enough to merely delete personal information. Deleted information remains on your hard drive and can be readily accessed by a computer savvy identity thief. Make sure you use one of the special programs that are available that will effectively remove the information from your hard drive.

3

DANGER ON THE COMPUTER AND WHAT TO DO IF YOU ARE THE VICTIM OF IDENTITY THEFT

S ometimes it is hard to remember what life was like without personal computers. E mail, shopping on line and surfing the net are only three of the uses of personal computers that are taken for granted in our everyday lives. But as much as computers have enriched our lives, they have also made us much more vulnerable to identity theft. The first step in reducing your vulnerability to identity theft through your computer is learning where you are vulnerable. However, assessing your risk is not enough. Unfortunately, there is nothing you can do to guarantee that you will not become a victim of identity theft, so it is also important to know what to do if you become an identity theft victim.

Spyware

The Good—The *I Spy* television series that ran from 1965 through 1968 and starred Bill Cosby and Robert Culp.

The Bad—The *I Spy* movie released in 2002 starring Eddie Murphy and Owen Wilson.

The Ugly—Spyware, computer software that can be used to gather and remove confidential information from your computer without your knowledge.

Everything you do online, including your passwords, may be vulnerable to spyware. Spyware can put you in great danger of becoming a victim of identity theft. To make the problem even worse, some forms of spyware can be installed on your computer from a remote location without the identity thief ever having physical access to your computer. You would think that it would be difficult for the average person to find spyware, but it is not. Typically it is used by employers monitoring employees' computer use and parents who monitor their children's computer use. It has been rumored that sometimes it is even used by a not-too-trusting spouse who wants to know what his or her spouse is doing online. In addition, some file sharing programs also contain spyware. Sometimes this information is used merely to send you advertisements for products and services that may interest you. "Cookies" planted by the spyware can be used to monitor your Internet use. Although "cookies" invade your privacy, they may have no more insidious intention than to tailor advertising to your specific interests. Although spyware does invade your privacy, you may have actually agreed to have spyware installed on your computer when you went to a particular Web site and accepted that Web site's user agreement, which can be long and filled with fine print that hardly anyone reads. Unfortunately, identity thieves looking to steal your identity and maybe your money also use spyware.

What Can You Do About Spyware?

Sir Isaac Newton's Third Law of Motion was that for every action, there is an equal and opposite reaction. This also seems to apply to modern computer use (or misuse). For every spyware program there also are anti-spyware programs that can let you know if your computer has been infected by spyware. Interestingly enough, some spyware developers use anti-spyware software to test the effectiveness of their own spyware and to try to make it less vulnerable to detection.

Although remote installation of spyware occurs, many spyware programs must physically be installed on your computer, so it is important to be sure who repairs and services your computers.

Another way to protect yourself is through the installation of software programs that record every software installation that occurs on your computer.

If you use this software, you obviously want to keep it hidden so that someone attempting to install spyware on your computer would be unaware that they are actually being monitored.

Some anti-virus programs also work against spyware and they provide good additional, if not total, protection.

Finally, return to Sir Isaac Newton and add to his laws of motion, the axiom, "If you can't beat them, join them." Because spyware permits all your computer's activities to be recorded, one way of telling that your computer has been accessed by someone with spyware is to install your own spyware in order to determine what has been going on in your computer.

It's Not Always Good to Share

File sharing is a way for people to share music, computer software or games over the Internet. It is simple to do. You just download software that permits you to connect your computer to a network of other computers using the same software and you are off to the races. Unfortunately, there are some significant risks involved in file sharing. If you do not install the file sharing software properly, you may make your computer vulnerable to having personal information stored on your computer retrieved by an identity thief through spyware.

Just When You Thought It was Safe to Go Back to Your Computer

People are always interested in firsts. Charles Lindbergh was the first man to fly solo across the Atlantic Ocean. Neil Armstrong was the first man to set foot on the moon. And nineteen-year-old Drexel College student Van Dinh was the first person to be charged by the Securities and Exchange Commission with fraud involving both computer hacking and identity theft. I am sure his parents are quite proud.

Dinh's story began in late June of 2003 when he bought 9,120 put option contracts on Cisco stock at a strike price of fifteen dollars per share. The cost to Dinh for each option contract was ten dollars per contract, for a total of $91,200. Each put option gave him the right to sell one hundred shares of Cisco stock at fifteen dollars per share if the value of the Cisco stock fell to that price or below before the date of the put option contracts, which expired on July 19, 2003. For example, if the stock price fell to fourteen dollars per share,

Dinh's ability to sell the shares at $15 per share according to the put option contracts would have resulted in a profit of $912,000. And if the stock fell even further, this highly speculative investment would have paid off even more handsomely. There was only one problem: With nine days to go before the expiration date of his Cisco put option contracts, the stock was trading at nineteen dollars per share, which meant that if that price level were maintained, his put option contracts would be worthless at their expiration.

According to the FBI, instead of just taking the potential loss, Dinh concocted an elaborate computer hacking and identity theft scheme to bail himself out. What Dinh needed were victims upon whom he could unload his soon to be worthless put option contracts. The first step was to find those victims. Dinh did this by going online to the investment analysis Web site stockcharts.com's stock-charting forum. Using the name Stanley Hirsch, Dinh e-mailed a message to at least 50 stockchart.com members asking if any of them maintained their own Web sites. When a Massachusetts investor responded to the e-mail, the first step in the fraud had been completed. By replying to Dinh's seemingly innocuous e-mail inquiry, the Massachusetts investor provided Dinh with the investor's personal e-mail address. The next day, Dinh, now using the name Tony T. Riechert contacted the unwary investor by e-mail and invited him to participate in a beta test of a new stock-charting tool. Beta testing is a common practice in the software development world by which individuals are solicited by companies to try out new versions of computer programs being developed as the companies try to get the "bugs" out of them. Continuing to swallow the bait, the Massachusetts investor accepted the invitation and downloaded the purported stock-charting software through a link in the e-mail message.

Unfortunately, the program was actually just a ruse known in the computer world as a "Trojan horse" that contained a number of keystroke-logging spyware programs. A "Trojan horse" is a computer program containing harmful codes hidden within an apparently harmless program. In this instance, a number of keystroke logging spyware programs were within the "Trojan horse". Keystroke-logging spyware programs, as I described earlier, permit an Internet user at one location to monitor all the keystrokes of another unsuspecting Internet user at a different location. Talk about food for paranoids! When the keystroke logging program known as "The Beast" was lodged in the Massachusetts investor's computer, Dinh simply had to wait and monitor his victim's computer use. From there, he found the last pieces of critical information necessary for his scam—the victim's password and login information for the victim's online brokerage account with TD Waterhouse.

On July 11, 2003, with only eight days left before the expiration of his Cisco put option contracts, Dinh hacked into his victim's TD Waterhouse account and made a series of Cisco option buy orders using up almost all the available cash in the victim's account. These buy orders were, in turn, executed on the Chicago Board Options Exchange and filled with options sold from Dinh's account, thereby avoiding a significant loss by Dinh. Four days later, the Massachusetts investor, shocked to see that his brokerage account had been raided, notified the Securities and Exchange Commission.

FBI and SEC investigators did not take long to trace the relevant e-mails. The e-mail from Tony Riechert was found to have come from Lockdown Corporation, a company that provides, in the words of the FBI, an "anonymizing" service to its customers that permits the true identity of the original sender of the e-mail to be hidden. Lockdown Corporation cooperated with the investigators and provided information that showed that the initiator of the Tony Riechert e-mail also had gone to the TD Waterhouse Web site and a hacker Web site that provided access to keystroke-logging spyware programs. The noose was tightening. Further investigation led to an Australian Internet service provider as well as e-mail servers in Ireland and Germany. Ultimately, the electronic trail led to Van Dinh who cooperated with investigators and provided SEC attorneys with information and documentation connecting him to the crimes.

The Lesson

The lesson could be the old one that crime does not pay. For Van Dinh, he was promptly caught; plus, his scheme only served, at best, to reduce the extent of his losses. However, for the rest of us the lesson is first to be aware that "Trojan horses" and keystroke-logging spyware programs exist. These invasions of your personal information cannot harm you unless you invite them in. Keep your virus software constantly updated. It is a good practice to be wary of downloadable programs offered from e-mail, forums or advertisements if you are not absolutely positive that they are legitimate. The lesson for brokerage houses is to maintain better security. Software is available that is able to detect changes in patterns of account holders or sudden, large liquidation of funds. The Patriot Act, enacted in the wake of the attacks of September 11, 2001, will also serve to help investors through its requirements of cross-referencing of personal information by financial service providers.

Wi-Fi: Something New to Worry About

Advances in computer technology are great. Unfortunately, they also often bring with them opportunities for identity theft. Starbucks is a very successful company. One of the perks of being a Starbucks customer is that they provide wireless Internet access in their stores so people can sit back, drink some expensive coffee and search the Internet. The way wireless Internet service, or Wi-Fi, works is by sending Web pages over radio waves to computers that have wireless capabilities. It is easy for technologically sophisticated identity thieves to hack into the computers of customers who are using their laptops at wireless access points often referred to as Internet "hot spots." Savvy hackers can join the network and access the information contained within the computers of users of the system. Wi-Fi is found more and more at malls, bookstores and even at McDonald's restaurants. Securing your laptop computer from hackers while using Wi-Fi facilities is complex and particularly difficult for the relatively unsophisticated technology user who often is also unlikely to keep his or her computer security and virus protections up-to-date.

Tip *Any computer that has wireless capabilities should also have security software installed at the same time.*

Stories

A Towering Problem

It is important to be sure that any company with which you do business protects your personal information; however, sometimes the assurances of those companies mean little. The FTC recently brought a complaint against Tower Records. The company claimed that it used state of the art technology to safeguard the personal information of customers. However, the security system it used permitted online users of its Web site to access personal information about other Tower customers. According to the FTC, this flaw in the security system was easy to fix, but Tower failed to do so until it was compelled by a formal complaint of the FTC that was settled in April 2004. In this case, as with all FTC settlements, Tower did not admit that it did anything wrong and agreed not to do it again.

We Regret to Inform You

It is not enough for you to protect yourself from identity theft. Any company with which you do business that has personal information about you is a potential victim of identity theft. In March 2004, GMAC notified 200,000 of its customers that their personal information might have been compromised (a euphemism for "possibly stolen") following the theft of two laptop computers used by GMAC employees that were stolen from an employee's car. Although the data stored on the particular laptop computers was protected by password access technology, the data itself was not encrypted as a further prudent security measure. The data itself was extremely sensitive material including, names, addresses, birth dates, and Social Security numbers of GMAC customers. This security breach is not uncommon in an era when employees may take work home on their laptops.

It is not even just the companies with which you do business that should con cern you. It is also the companies with which they do business and with which they may share your personal information. In 2003, the Bank of Rhode Island contacted 43,000 of its customers to warn them that their personal information, including Social Security numbers, may have been compromised. A laptop computer used by an employee of Fiserv, Inc., a company with which the Bank of Rhode Island did business, was stolen. This laptop computer contained sensitive personal information about Bank of Rhode Island customers.

California, a state that has often been the leader in identity protection laws, has had a law since 2003 that requires any business that has had a breach of its computer security to notify its customers. Similar laws are expected to be passed in other states, although it would be even better if companies paid greater attention to preventing their systems from being improperly accessed in the first place.

Keys to Identity Theft

It was bad enough that two Wells Fargo employees left the car keys in the ignition of their unlocked rental car during a stop at a Missouri gas station convenience store while they went inside in February 2004. When they came out, their Ford Mustang was gone. But also gone with the car was the laptop computer that they had left unattended in the trunk of the car. The computer contained the names, addresses and Social Security numbers of thousands of

Wells Fargo mortgage customers. The car was retrieved less than a week later, but the computer was gone. A password was required to access the personal information stored on the computer, but the simplicity of that task to a computer savvy identity thief left Wells Fargo's mortgage customers in substantial danger of identity theft.

Tip *Ask any company with which you do about their policy for the security and protection of personal information, including whether your information is encrypted in their computers. If their answers do not satisfy you, take your business elsewhere.*

If You Can't Trust Your Lawyer, Whom Can You Trust?

If you can't trust your own lawyer, whom can you trust? My grandmother, the same one who used to say that she could keep secrets but that the people to whom she told them could not, used to refer to me as her grandson, "the liar." I used to try to correct her, telling her that the name of my profession was pronounced "lawyer," to which she always responded, "Don't correct me, I know what I'm saying." I think my grandmother was kidding. I hope my grandmother was kidding, but many people do consider lawyers just a bunch of liars. The case of Iric Vonn Spears, unfortunately, does little to dispel that impression. Iric Vonn Spears was an attorney who, having access to the personal information of his client Reginald Dalton, used that information to steal Dalton's identity and buy a home and open credit card accounts. The house of cards tumbled when the real Dalton was contacted by the bank that held the mortgage on the home purchased by Iric Vonn Spears using the name of Reginald Dalton, telling him that the mortgage was being foreclosed. Iric Vonn Spears was convicted of grand theft, mortgage fraud, identity fraud and forgery. He was sentenced to ten years in prison.

What to Do If You Are a Victim of Identity Theft

1. Put a fraud alert on your credit report. Under new federal law, fraud alerts take on an increased importance. If you think that you might be the victim of identity theft, you can have a fraud alert placed upon your credit

---

report at the credit reporting agencies. The alert stays on your report for up to ninety days but can be extended for up to seven years. When a fraud alert has been put on your credit report, you are entitled to a second free credit report during that year in order to monitor your credit for further irregularities. In the past, people placing a fraud alert on their credit reports found that to be effective, they had to call each of the three major credit reporting agencies to have fraud alerts independently placed on each company's record. Now under FACT (the federal Fair and Accurate Credit Transactions Act), all you need to do is call one of the credit reporting agencies and they are required to notify the other two to place the fraud alert on your file.

2. Go to the Federal Trade Commission web site or the back of this book to obtain the FTC's ID Theft Affidavit and use it to report the crime.

3. Contact all your creditors by phone and then follow up with a letter sent by certified mail, return receipt requested. See Chapter 15, "Form Letters," for a sample. Get new credit cards with new account numbers. Change your PIN number and your passwords.

4. Close tainted accounts. When opening new accounts with these creditors, use a password that is not easily connected with you. A word to the wise: Do not use your mother's maiden name, or to be particularly safe, do not even use my mother's maiden name. People think that their mother's maiden name is difficult to find. It is not. It is on your birth certificate, a public record.

5. When you close accounts, make sure that the accounts are designated as being closed at the customer's request due to theft so that when information is transmitted to the credit reporting bureau, it is clear that the problems are not of your doing.

6. Ask your creditors to notify each of the credit reporting agencies to remove erroneous and fraudulent information from your file.

7. If your checks are stolen, promptly notify your bank and have the account closed immediately. If your checking account is accessed by checks with forged signatures, you obviously have not authorized the withdrawals and should not be held responsible for money stolen from your account. However, if you neglect to monitor your account and fail to promptly notify your bank when there is an irregularity in your account or your

checks are lost or stolen, you may be held partially responsible for your losses. It is not even necessary to have your checks physically stolen for you to become a victim. An identity thief armed with your name, checking account number, and bank routing information can use one of a number of inexpensive computer software programs to create checks for your account.

8. Contact the various check verification companies and ask that they, in turn, contact retailers who use their services telling them not to accept checks from your accounts that have been accessed by identity thieves. Check verification services are companies that maintain databases of bad check writers. Retailers using their services contact the verification service's database before accepting checks. Among the companies that do check verification are CellCharge, CheckCare, and CrossCheck.

9. File a report with the police both where the fraud occurred and where you live. You may find police departments reluctant to accept your report, sometimes for technical legal jurisdictional reasons. Politely insist that they at least accept your report. Remind them that credit bureaus will prevent fraudulent accounts from appearing on your credit report if you can provide a police report. Give the police officer taking the report as much documentation as you have to support your claim, including the ID Theft Affidavit approved by the Federal Trade Commission that appears later in this book. When a police report has been filed, send a copy of it to each of the three major credit-reporting agencies.

10. Be proactive. Contact your creditors where you have tainted accounts and get a written statement from each of them indicating that the account accessed by an identity theft has been closed and that the charges made to the accounts are fraudulent. Request that they initiate a fraud investigation. Find out what you are required to do to advance the investigation, such as providing them with a police report. A sample letter to your creditor requesting such a statement from your creditors is included in Chapter 15. These letters can be very helpful, particularly if the credit reporting bureaus mistakenly resubmit the fraudulent charges on your credit report. Remember to get a written copy of your creditor's completed investigation.

11. Send copies of your creditors' completed investigations to each of the three credit reporting agencies. Ask them to send you a copy of your updated credit report in order to confirm that any erroneous and fraudulent information has been removed from your file.

12. If fraudulent charges do appear on your credit report, notify the credit reporting bureaus in writing that you dispute the information and request that such information be removed from your file. A sample letter is included in Chapter 15.

4

YOUR SOCIAL SECURITY NUMBER—AN IDENTITY THIEF'S LUCKY NUMBER

Allow an identity thief access to your Social Security number and in a very short time you will be victimized. Armed with your Social Security number an identity thief can readily access your bank accounts and other assets as well as establish credit and run up debts in your name. Protecting your Social Security number requires great diligence.

Driver's License

In 1996, the Federal Immigration Reform Act made it mandatory for each of the states to obtain the Social Security number of every applicant for a driver's license in an effort to reduce illegal immigration. Unfortunately, a side effect of this legislation was that more states started using your Social Security number as your license number. Despite efforts in Congress to specifically outlaw the use of Social Security numbers as driver's license numbers, the practice continues in a number of states. However, most states will permit you to use another random number for your license number unless you specifically request that your Social Security number be used as your license number, a request that you should never under any circumstances make. Get a different number for your license number. Many health insurance cards also use your Social Security number as the identifying number on the card. Request a new number there too.

The Federal Drivers Privacy Protection Act bans states from providing your personal information to marketers without your permission. Do not give this permission. It would only make you more vulnerable to identity theft. Although the law prevents the individual state departments of motor vehicles from providing your personal information to marketers, they are allowed to give this information to law enforcement agencies, courts, government agencies, insurance companies and others with legitimate needs for this information.

When and Where Must You Provide Your Social Security Number?

There are a few scenarios where you must provide your Social Security number, including income tax returns, medical records, credit reports, loan applications, and driver's license applications (but remember not to use it as your driver's license number appearing on your license).

Should You Try to Get a New Social Security Number If Yours Has Been Used for Identity Theft?

I will give you the lawyer answer to this question, which is yes and no. Now isn't that helpful? On the one hand, having the Social Security Administration change your number will be an incredibly complicated thing to do. Its very complexity will bring with it the potential for future problems, particularly if there are gaps in the records of any of the legitimate entities that need and use your Social Security number for identification. The Social Security Administration is also very reluctant to issue new Social Security numbers because they are always a bit skeptical that rather than being a victim, you might be someone trying to establish new credit by ditching the old credit reports attached to your former number. However, if someone who has access to your Social Security number is stalking you or if you are a repeated victim of identity theft by someone who has your Social Security number, the Social Security Administration might be a bit more sympathetic. In any event, the Social Security Administration will not issue you a new Social Security number if you have filed for bankruptcy or your Social Security card was lost or stolen unless there is evidence that you have been the actual victim of identity theft.

Restrictions on the Use of Social Security Numbers

Recognizing the threat of identity theft presented by the prominent display of Social Security numbers, the federal government has taken a number of steps to reduce their use. The IRS no longer puts Social Security numbers on the pre-printed labels sent to taxpayers. The Social Security Administration itself has ceased using Social Security numbers in written communications wherever possible while the Treasury Department, as of January 2004, no longer includes Social Security numbers on Social Security checks. Unfortunately, Medicare cards continue to carry the Medicare recipient's name and Social Security number, thereby making Medicare-receiving senior citizens more susceptible to identity theft.

Not Even Safe After Death

Believe it or not, you can become the victim of identity theft even after your death. In fact, it may be easier to become a victim of identity theft after death. In order to obtain the Social Security number of a deceased person, a criminal simply goes to the Social Security Master Death Index, which can be easily accessed at no cost online, and enters the name of the deceased. Hit "Submit," and in a moment, the Social Security numbers and dates of birth for people with the name entered will appear. Identity thieves merely get names from the obituaries in the newspaper, go to the Social Security Master Death Index and get the information necessary to perform a quick identity theft before the credit reporting agencies, credit card companies or others are even aware that a death has occurred.

For years, pranksters still holding a grudge against former President Richard Nixon have used his Social Security number whenever required to provide a Social Security number but not wishing to cooperate. In order to check this out, I went to the Social Security Master Death Index and was able to get his Social Security number, which is 567-68-0515.

In the Navy

Fitness reports and evaluations are regularly generated forms in the Navy. In the past, these forms have routinely carried the Social Security number of the reporting senior officer. In 2004, however, the Navy issued an Administrative Message that permits the reporting senior officer to prepare the individual's copy of the fitness report or evaluation with "000-00-0000" appearing in the block on the form where the reporting senior officer's Social Security number would appear. The original form of the report or evaluation, which is filed with Naval Personnel Command, still will carry the reporting senior officer's Social Security number, but all other copies of the reports and evaluations will not carry the reporting senior officer's Social Security number.

Doctored Records

Medical offices are particularly attractive targets for identity thieves because of the abundant personal information, including your Social Security number, that is included in your office records. In 2004, Quest Diagnostics, a national company that performs medical laboratory tests such as blood and urine analysis, had its information illegally accessed and used to make fraudulent purchases, including a $42,100 Cadillac Escalade. A thief made these purchases by using personal information of Edward Smith, who had been a patient of Quest Diagnostics. Smith became aware of the theft of his identity when he received a letter from an automobile insurance company congratulating him on the recent purchase of the car. Smith, who used Quest Diagnostics for blood tests for high cholesterol may now have to worry about his blood pressure going up over the stress of his identity theft.

✒ Driving Miss Daisy to Identity Theft

The car salesman at Foreign Motors West in Natick, Massachusetts was having a good day when a New Yorker ordered not just one, but two BMW automobiles for $130,000. Fortunately for the real New Yorker, the Massachusetts con man posing as the New Yorker aroused the suspicion of the car dealership despite the fact that all his identification, including his driver's license appeared to be in good order. Specifically, the identity thief wanted the cars as soon as possible regardless of cost or color. An investigation led to the breaking of the news to the man whose identity had been stolen. He was not even aware that his identity had been stolen. When the con man came back to pick up the first of his cars, the police were waiting to arrest him. He was charged with conspiracy, identity theft, larceny by false pretenses, forgery and uttering.

New Definition of "Chutzpah"

"Chutzpah" is a Yiddish word, the short definition of which is "gall." However, a better definition is provided through the often-told story of the young man who, having killed both his father and mother, pleads for mercy before the court on the ground that he is an orphan. We now have a new definition of chutzpah and it involves Steven M. Gilroy. Gilroy, an Oregon man, was accused of identity theft in 2004 through his use of a West Linn, Oregon woman's credit cards for everything from a grill ornament for his car to $310 in court fines. And just what were those fines for? They were fines from a 2002 identity theft conviction that police say he paid with the Oregon woman's credit card.

❧ Hell Hath No Fury Like a Woman Scorned

Many people are familiar with the phrase, "Hell hath no fury like a woman scorned," but few know that it comes from the play *The Mourning Bride* by William Congreve, a British author of the late seventeenth and early eighteenth centuries. Interestingly enough, that same play also contains the line, "Music hath charms to soothe the savage breast." That is not a typo; the word is "breast," not "beast." I cannot even imagine what a savage breast is. I don't think it has anything to do with Janet Jackson and the half-time show at the 2004 Super Bowl, though. In any event, I thought about the first of the aforementioned phrases when I learned about the conviction of Carol Baldasare on fraud and identity theft charges after she stole the identities of her estranged husband and mother-in-law and ran up $2,800 in credit card bills in their names.

Workplace Identity Theft

Regardless of how vigilant you may be in your personal life maintaining the privacy of your Social Security number, your job may put you in jeopardy of identity theft. Employers must have access to the Social Security numbers of their employees. Phony employers seeking your Social Security number for identity theft purposes present obvious problems. Less obvious, however, is the risk you face from lax personal information security of some employers. Your employer's information security problems can easily become yours.

Looking for a Job

While not typically thought of as a threatening situation, online job postings can be fodder for identity thieves. There are many legitimate online employment companies, but even they can be scammed and list phony job descriptions for the purpose of luring people into becoming victims of identity theft. Monster.com has specifically warned its users that false job postings are used to collect sensitive, personal information from unwary job applicants. With a few simple precautions, however, you should be able to avoid becoming an identity theft victim through an online job listing. One thing to remember is that there is no need to send a prospective employer any information that is obviously unrelated to your obtaining employment. No employer needs to know your bank account numbers or credit card numbers, and certainly not your mother's maiden name. The tough call is when an employer asks for your Social Security number because it is legitimate for an employer to look at your credit report for employment purposes. The best and most prudent course of action is to ask if you can wait until a meeting in person with a prospective employer before providing that critical piece of information to anyone about whose legitimacy you have even the slightest concerns.

I Gave at the Office

Burglaries at the workplace are on the rise. And sometimes the thieves are not concerned with the money in your wallet. They want your identity. A purse left out in the open is fair game for the thief, who may grab a credit card, or even your driver's license, to aid in identity theft. This booty may be used by the thief directly or sold to another identity thief who just uses the services of such petty thieves. Be careful. Keep your purse or other personal information secured at all times. Employers should enact policies to restrict access to work areas by visitors and unauthorized persons unless authorized personnel accompany them.

Who Do You Trust?

Johnny Carson, long-time host of the *Tonight Show*, hosted a quiz show entitled *Who Do You Trust*. It probably should have been called *Whom Do You Trust*, although proper grammar is not a particularly highly valued commodity in television. In any event, in April 2004, members of the San Diego Firefighters Local 145 Union were wondering who or whom they could trust when their offices were burglarized over a weekend. Curiously enough, an old computer was taken while newer, more valuable, computers were left untouched. The old computer that was taken, however, was the one in which personal information, including Social Security numbers, of the union members was stored, raising the possibility that someone on the inside may have been responsible.

Another Inside Job

Andrew Dorsey, a former employee of First USA Bank conspired with David Fletcher in late 2000 and early 2001 in the theft of personal financial information and account numbers from twenty credit card customers of First USA Bank, now known as Bank One. Both were convicted of identity theft.

Disgruntled Employee

We constantly hear stories of disgruntled employees, people discontented at work which brings up the question, if a person is satisfied with his or her job, he or she may be considered to be contented, so why do you never hear about a "gruntled" employee who would be the opposite of a disgruntled employee? In any event, Steven Sutcliffe definitely qualified as a disgruntled employee of Global Crossing following his firing in September of 2001. The angry Sutcliffe not only posted threats to specific Global Crossing employees online, but he also put the addresses and Social Security numbers of around two thousand employees and former employees of Global Crossing on the Internet. He was sentenced to prison following his conviction on identity theft and other charges.

Temporary Worker—Long Time Problem

With so many businesses having control of sensitive personal information today, it is imperative that businesses become much more cognizant of security measures to protect that information. An area of particular concern is temporary workers who may not be screened as carefully as full-time hired employees. In California, Anthony Johnson was convicted of obtaining personal information through his job as a temporary worker at an insurance company. He used the information to facilitate identity theft to the tune of $764,000, which is actually more of a symphony than a tune.

Tip *Employers working with a Temporary Office Help agency should inquire as to the extent of the screening and background checks the Temporary Office Help agency performs on its employees. You also may wish to limit the access of temporary workers to personal information in your records.*

Another Horror Story

For more than three years, New Yorker Phillip Cummings was one of the key figures in an identity theft ring that may have victimized more than thirty thousand people. This was an organized operation in which the sensitive personal financial information of its victims was sold by Cummings to a group of twenty Nigerians living in the New York City area who used this information to facilitate identity theft. Cummings received approximately thirty dollars for access to each credit report he passed on to the Nigerians. Using the information contained in the credit reports, the identity thieves obtained access to bank accounts and credit cards of their unwary victims with total losses in the millions of dollars.

The weak link that allowed Cummings to easily get the identifying information of thousands of people without leaving his desk was a credit prompter box which is used by legitimate automobile dealers and others to obtain quick access to credit reports at each of the three major credit reporting agencies. The key to accessing these credit reports is having the right user name and password. According to the criminal complaint against Cummings, "Any Help Desk representative has access to confidential passwords and subscriber codes of TCI (Teladata, the maker of the equipment) client companies that would have enabled that employee to download credit reports from all three Credit Bureaus." Even after Cummings left Teladata less than a year after being involved in the scam, the scam itself continued with Cummings still able to pass on to his co-conspirators the company codes previously provided. Even after he left Teledata Cummings' employee password was used by the identity thieves to whom Cummings sold this information to continue to log into Teledata's systems.

As so often is the case, it was the thieves' own greed that did them in. Between 2001 and 2002, the identity thieves used Ford Motor Company's name and code to get the credit reports on fifteen thousand victims. When someone noticed unusual account activity, the account was closed and authorities were notified that something was wrong. A further investigation by Equifax of another, later batch of credit reports led law enforcement to a telephone number in New Rochelle, New York, which was the source of the credit report requests, usually initiated by someone identified in the report requests as using the initials "MM." On October 29, 2002, it was an early "trick or treat" for federal law enforcement authorities that raided the New Rochelle location used by Cummings' partners in crime. There they found computers and other equipment that told the story of the crime.

Preventing Identity Theft at Work

1. Anyone who has access to your workspace may have access to your computer and the information contained therein. Fellow workers, visitors, business support personnel or, at worst, burglars can get at the information in your computer unless you protect it. Use passwords for sensitive information. Turn off the computer when you are not using it, or set the computer to automatically log out after a few minutes of non-use.

2. Use encryption programs.

3. Do not have your passwords stored in your software for frequently visited Web sites. Log them in each time you visit a site. You may wish to change your password periodically. If you do, mix letters and numbers to make your password less vulnerable. And, of course, it is important to have passwords you can remember.

4. When you replace your computer, make sure that the hard drive on your old computer has all the information stored there permanently erased. Merely deleting information on your computer does not permanently erase data. There are a number of inexpensive software programs that will permanently remove information from your hard drive.

Higher Education and Identity Theft

You would think that the best and brightest minds at our colleges and universities would be particularly cognizant of the problem of identity theft and the importance of using the latest technology to maintain the security of sensitive student data such as their Social Security numbers—but you would be wrong.

School of Thieves

It is taking too long for many institutions to realize that access to Social Security numbers is the first step toward someone becoming victimized by identity theft.

You would think that our institutions of higher learning would be able to figure that out, but unfortunately too many colleges and universities still use Social Security numbers on student identification cards, registration for classes, class rosters, and for posting of grades.

In 2000, a Washington University philosophy professor (apparently not well versed in Ethics, a basic philosophy course) was sent to prison for stealing the Social Security numbers of students and utilizing the numbers in a credit card fraud scheme.

In 2003, a computer criminal hacked into the main computers of the University of Texas and harvested 55,000 Social Security numbers of students, faculty, and staff.

Fool Me Once

According to the old saying, "Fool me once, shame on you. Fool me twice, shame on me." Hackers accessed the University of Texas's computers in October 2003. Names and Social Security numbers were taken, but a mere five months later more than 55,000 names and Social Security numbers were again lost to hackers of the University of Texas's computers.

Oops

An employee of the California State University at Monterey Bay mistakenly moved information on close to 3,000 applicants to a computer folder that was not secure. The employee unwittingly put this information out over the Internet where it was seen more than 100 times before the mistake was caught and remedied.

In January 2004, campus officials at New York University learned that a number of university mailing lists containing names, birth dates, addresses, telephone numbers, e-mail addresses, and even some Social Security numbers, for more than 2,000 current students, alumni, and professors were mistakenly posted on an easily accessible campus website.

In March 2004, a list of more than 11,000 MIT employees' Social Security numbers and MIT identification numbers were found to have been posted on the Internet for more than six months. It does not take a rocket scientist to realize that this is not a good thing. The information was accidentally placed on the Internet, but the threat of identity theft was just as real as if an identity thief had posted that personal information.

❧ Not Only in America

Our neighbors to the north are not immune from identity theft. An eighty-nine-year-old Calgary woman did not know the title to her million dollar tract of undeveloped land located in one of the main business areas of the city had been stolen from her until a mortgage broker inquired as to whether she had recently sold it. The scheme to cheat the property owner and a mortgage company fell apart when one of the criminals bounced a $2,000 check to a property appraiser after taking out a half-a-million-dollar mortgage on the property. The mortgage broker then learned that the man, who had been presented as the owner of the property, was actually a homeless person drawn into the scam by the criminal masterminds who through false identification cards were able to transfer the property and then mortgage it. Elizabeth Jean Costello, the true owner of the property ultimately had her title to the property restored as well as having her legal fees reimbursed. The true losers in this case were the taxpayers of the province of Alberta when its Land Titles Insurance Fund ended up refunding money to the victimized mortgage company, much of which was never recovered.

5

CRIMINAL IDENTITY THEFT, TAXES—AND MORE ARRESTING PROBLEMS

Identity theft can take on repercussions that you can hardly imagine. You can be arrested for a crime committed by someone who has stolen your identity. You can become an identity theft victim merely by filing your tax returns or what you think are your tax returns. You can even be sued by companies with which you do business seeking compensation for fraudulent accounts even after it has been established that you are the victim of identity theft.

Criminal Misidentification

Usually, when you hear a professional athlete discussing his contract say "Its not about the money," there is one thing of which you can be sure — it's about the money. But when it comes to identity theft, it often is not about the money. The problems encountered by someone whose identity has been stolen by a criminal, who then commits crimes in the name of the identity theft victim, are substantial. They involve much more than money.

Hoisted with His Own Petard

James Perry, being concerned that his four drunk driving convictions in Florida would interfere with his application for a Connecticut driver's license, stole the identity of his neighbor, Robert Kowalski. Perry managed to get a Connecticut driver's license and credit cards in the name of Robert Kowalski. Everything was going fine for Perry until he was arrested on a minor disorderly conduct charge. In accordance with standard operating procedure, Kowalski's name was put through a background check for outstanding warrants, and the search indicated that Robert Kowalski was a convicted sex offender who had failed to register in Connecticut as required by state law. Suddenly James Perry decided that it was better to be James Perry than Robert Kowalski and he confessed to his crime. An FBI fingerprint check confirmed his true identity, and he was promptly charged with criminal impersonation.

That's Me. That's Me. That's Not Me.

Like James Perry, Theodore Ceja should have been more careful when he stole the identity of Jose A. Fabela. When he was stopped for a simple speeding infraction in Indiana, Theodore Ceja presented a driver's license in the name of Jose A. Fabela. The subsequent customary criminal computer check on Jose A. Fabela turned up a warrant for his arrest from Texas on charges of attempted murder. At this point, Theodore Ceja was only too happy to provide Indiana authorities with documentation proving his true identity. Better charges of suspicion of identity theft and false informing than attempted murder.

Arrest Gone to Pot

During a routine traffic stop in Marietta, Ohio, police found that Shaun Saunders had eight pounds of marijuana in his possession. Bail was set at $15,000 and Saunders was promptly released on bail when someone came to court and put up the full bail amount in cash. When Saunders failed to appear for a preliminary hearing, he was indicted by a grand jury. A few months later, police in Bluefield, Virginia, notified Marietta police that they had Shaun Saunders in custody. In fact, they were holding Shaun Saunders. The only problem was that FBI fingerprint identification confirmed that the man who had been stopped and arrested by Ohio police was not Shaun Saunders, whose wallet with identifying information had been stolen a year earlier.

And You Thought You Had a Bad Day

For eighteen years Darryl Hunt was incarcerated in a North Carolina prison after being convicted of a murder that he did not commit. He was finally released on Christmas Eve 2003, after being exonerated through the use of DNA evidence whereupon Darryl Hunt found out that his bad luck was not over. While he was in prison, someone stole his identity and racked up more than $5,200 in debts. Hunt only became aware of the problem when he was notified that a $1,400 claim had been made against his income tax refund due to an unpaid loan. An identity thief took out the loan while Hunt was serving time in the Piedmont Correctional Institution in Salisbury, North Carolina. When Hunt investigated the matter, he found an additional $3,800 of bogus debt run up in his name while he was in prison. Police traced the identity theft to someone who improperly applied for and received an identification card from the North Carolina Division of Motor Vehicles, using Darryl Hunt's name, birth date, and a Winston-Salem address.

It's Not Just the Money

One of the more insidious forms of identity theft occurs when an identity thief uses your identity not just to steal from you or harm your credit, but commits crimes using your name. Derek Bond, a 72-year-old British retired charity worker was arrested and held in a South African jail for two weeks in February 2003 awaiting extradition to the United States on an FBI arrest warrant. The FBI did not admit that it had made a mistake in detaining Derek Bond until the real criminal, Derek Sikes, was arrested in Las Vegas. Derek Sikes may have been using Derek Bond's identity for as long as 14 years before the unfortunate Derek Bond became aware of the theft of his good name.

But as bad as Derek Bond's case was, Malcolm Byrd's is even worse. Malcolm Byrd's troubles began in 1998 when he read in the local newspaper that he had been arrested on drug charges. He promptly contacted the police who quickly determined that Byrd was the victim of identity theft. The newspaper even printed a retraction, clarifying the situation. You would think that that would be the end of the story. But unfortunately for Malcolm Byrd, it was not.

Barely four months after he thought he had straightened out the matter, he was arrested on the same drug charges. He was released later that day when it again became apparent to the police that Malcolm Byrd was the victim, not the perpetrator. But his problems continued. Over the next five years, his problems continued to mount. First, he was fired when his employer mistakenly accused him of misrepresenting his criminal record. Then he was denied unemployment benefits because of his criminal record that, in truth, never existed. His driver's license was suspended for unpaid traffic tickets he never received. One by one, Malcolm Byrd managed to correct all these mistakes, but his own name continues to haunt him. In March 2003 while at home with his children, he was arrested and charged with cocaine possession with intent to distribute. Despite his fervent efforts, the Rock County Wisconsin sheriff's officers remained convinced that he was the man they wanted. They continued to remain convinced for the two days he had to stay in jail until the proof of his true identity was established, at least for the moment, and he was released.

What Should You Do If You Are the Victim of Criminal Identity Theft?

1. Act as soon as you become aware of the problem. Hire a lawyer and contact the police and the District Attorney's office to straighten out the matter. File a report indicating that you are the victim of identity theft. It will be necessary for you to confirm your own identity through photographs and fingerprints. In addition, show your driver's license, passport, or any other identification that you might have that contains your photograph, to law enforcement authorities.

2. Get a letter from the District Attorney explaining the situation to have available if you are ever stopped for a traffic violation and your record is checked. The state of Virgina has an Identity Theft Passport Program within the Virginia Attorney General's office. Through this program, anyone whose identity has been appropriated by someone who uses it in the commission of a crime can, upon proving their identity, receive an Identity Theft Passport from the Attorney General. The Identity Theft

Passport protects them and confirms their true identity if there is a question about their criminal responsibility.

3. Make sure your criminal record is expunged.

4. Consider changing your name.

5. Consider changing your Social Security number.

Taxes and Identity Theft

Taxes and identity theft seem like a match made in hell. Taxes are bad enough, but piling on identity theft compounds the misery. Whether it is being victimized by a tax preparing identity thief or falling prey to an identity theft scam that uses phony forms to lure you into providing your Social Security number and other sensitive information, the result is the same—trouble.

Tax Preparation and Identity Theft

Preparing your income tax return can be taxing enough. Becoming a victim of identity theft in the process seems like cruel and unusual punishment. Many people go to commercial tax preparers who often set up in large rooms in malls or sections of larger stores. At times, the privacy and security of your information is not as protected as it should be. Identity thieves lurking in these places can see documents and information on computer screens. The solution is to always be conscious of maintaining the privacy of your documents and information. Of course, this applies when you are discarding any documents that you might have used to prepare your tax returns. Your trash may be treasure to an identity thief. Thoroughly shred any financial worksheets or documents used to help prepare your income taxes when discarding them.

IRS Scam

In this scam, the identity thief sends you a phony e-mail that says it is from the IRS asking for personal information as a part of an audit.

By now, you should know the drill. Do not give it out. The IRS does not use e-mail to contact taxpayers.

Multiple Tax Returns

Most people have a hard enough time filing one federal income tax return per year. Tonya Nicole Williams managed to file seventeen federal income tax returns online for the tax years of 2000 and 2001. Unfortunately, they were fraudulent returns filed in an attempt to steal $67,000 in refund money from the IRS. Williams used personal information she had obtained from people for whom she had previously legitimately prepared tax returns to further her scheme. Ultimately, she was convicted of identity theft, bank fraud, and the filing of false income tax returns.

Another Taxing Form of Identity Theft

A New York band of identity thieves used change of address cards to divert their victims' mail, and using personal information such as their victims' Social Security numbers was able to cash their victims' income tax refunds, steal money from their victim's bank accounts through ATM machines, and get credit cards. They ran up thousands of dollars of fraudulent charges over a period of two years before law enforcement was able to put together the pieces of the puzzle in early 2003. Because the identity thefts were traced back to mail fraud through the use of change of address forms, federal postal investigators joined the hunt to find the common thread that joined the victims. Postal inspector Richard Tracy was the first to notice what it was that victims from the Bronx, Westchester, Rockland, and Putnam, New York all had in common. They all had their income tax returns prepared by the same office of H & R Block in White Plains, New York in 2000 and 2001. From that information, the trail eventually led to a former crooked office manager at that office who used his access to customers' names, Social Security numbers, and other personal information contained in their files to steal the identities of those customers.

More Tax Scams

The forms that the unfortunate victims received looked just like IRS forms. One form was titled "W-9095, Application Form For Certificate

Status/Ownership for Withholding Tax." The instructions in a letter, supposedly from the victims' banks, said that in order to prevent the automatic withholding of 31% of the interest on the account, the form must be completed and faxed back to the bank within seven days. But the fax number to which the victims sent the faxed forms was not the fax number of the bank. The information required by the form was personal information such as mother's maiden name, passport number, PIN numbers, and bank account numbers that would never be requested by the IRS. Anyone completing these forms soon became an identity theft victim. The best course of action for anyone receiving a form that seeks personal information is to scrutinize it carefully, and if you have any questions, contact the financial institution sending the form to confirm that it is legitimate.

Tax Scam on Non-Resident Aliens

The 2.5 million non-resident aliens who receive taxable income in the United States from sources such as stock dividends or bonds from American companies have become a target of identity thieves. According to the IRS, these thieves pose as IRS agents when they contact their victims asking for personal information that they use to facilitate identity theft. The ruse for obtaining the sensitive information is that the non-resident alien will be taxed in the United States at the maximum rate unless they provide the requested information. A criminally altered IRS Form W-8BEN is then sent to the alien asking for personal information such as birth date, Social Security number, passport number, bank information, and even information on other members of their family. The legitimate IRS Form W-8BEN that is used to determine a non-resident alien's foreign status and whether that person is subject to American tax withholding does not require any personal information other than the Social Security number. In addition to the request for extensive personal information, another way to tell that the form is legitimate is the source of the form. The IRS never sends out these forms; the real ones only come from the alien's American financial institutions.

Identity Theft and Investments

Frank Gruttadauria was a successful investment broker who handled millions of dollars on behalf of his wealthy clients. He was also an identity thief who was convicted in 2002 of securities fraud, wire fraud, bank fraud, and identity theft that made his clients much less wealthy. His easy access to not only his clients' personal information but also their actual accounts made his crimes both easier to accomplish and more frightening to people who already feel quite vulnerable. The Ohio-based Gruttadauria stole $125 million dollars from his client's accounts, shifting money from one client's account to another and all the time keeping plenty for himself.

Tip *Read your monthly brokerage account statements carefully. Look for anything out of the ordinary. Make sure your broker explains anything to you that you do not understand. Get a second opinion. A certified financial planner may be able to better review your statement for you and perhaps, as an added bonus, even make suggestions that may include tax advice pertaining to your investments with expertise that your broker may not necessarily possess.*

Also, ask the branch manager of the investment company with which you do business about its policies for reviewing and overseeing the actions of their individual brokers. This should be done on a regular basis.

Deadly Results of Identity Theft

In 1999 Liam Youens hired an Internet-based investigation and information service known as Docusearch.com to provide information on a woman named Amy Lynn Boyer. For a fee of only $45 dollars he was able to obtain Ms. Boyer's Social Security number from Docusearch, which had obtained this information from a "credit header" through a credit-reporting agency. A "credit header" is the basic information found at the top of a person's credit report. It contains not just the person's name and address, but also, most importantly, that person's Social Security number, the key to so much more information. Docusearch also provided Youens with Boyer's home address as well as her work address. The work address was obtained through a "pretext" telephone call in which Amy Lynn

Boyer was contacted by telephone by a person who lied about the true purpose of the call in order to get Boyer to disclose her place of employment. Pretexting is often done to obtain information used to defraud the victim. In this case, the ultimate result of the pretexting was the death of Amy Lynn Boyer. On October 15, 1999, Liam Youens went to Amy Lynn Boyer's workplace where he waited until she left the building, whereupon he shot and killed her and then killed himself. The police investigation of the crime found that Youens actually maintained a Web site in which there were references to stalking and killing Amy Lynn Boyer. The estate of Amy Lynn Boyer sued Docusearch, arguing that people who obtain and sell personal information are responsible to the people whose personal information is sold if they are harmed as a result of the sale of that information. The New Hampshire Supreme Court ruled that "The threats posed by stalking and identity theft lead us to conclude that the risk of criminal misconduct is sufficiently foreseeable so that an investigator has a duty to exercise reasonable care in disclosing a third person's personal information to a client... This is especially true when, as in this case, the investigator does not know the client or the client's purpose in seeking the information."[1]

❧ Jury Duty

Comedian Norm Crosby said that he did not like the idea of trusting his fate to twelve people who were not smart enough to get out of jury duty. Jury duty is a civic duty, like voting, that we should embrace. At least, that is the theory. Unfortunately it would be naïve to fail to recognize that many people consider jury duty an annoyance and a disturbance of their everyday lives to be avoided whenever possible. Identity thieves know this. One identity theft scam involves the thief posing as a court worker placing telephone calls to people. During those phone calls, he tells his victims that the records indicate that the person being called has failed to report for jury duty. The identity thief then asks the potential victims to provide their Social Security numbers and other personal information. And then, as they say, the game begins.

Urban Myth

A persistent rumor making the rounds says that the electronically encrypted key cards used by many hotels as hotel room keys are a source of identity theft. The rumor says that encoded on your key card is your name, your home address, your hotel room number, your check-in and check-out date, as well as your credit card number. According to the rumor, when you turn in your key at the end of your stay, you run the risk of unscrupulous employees using portable scanners to take that information, most notably your name and credit card number, off the key card and use it to your detriment. The basis for the rumor comes from an alert issued by Pasadena, California Police Detective Sergeant Kathryn Jorge according to www.mybend.com, who is quoted as saying, "In years past, existing software would prompt the user (employee) for information input. If the employee was unaware of hotel police dictating that such information not be entered, it could have ended up on the card in error." However, she also went on to say, "Since this subject came up, experiments on newer cards have failed to duplicate the problem." Hotel operators say that no personal information that would pose an identity theft risk is used on key cards today, and some say there never was. They say that the only information that ever was imbedded in the key card was the name of the hotel guest, the number of the room, the check-in date, and the check-out date. This last bit of information keeps the key card from being used on the particular room after the guest's hotel stay is completed.

Stories

Identity theft can occur even before birth. It can happen to senators and district attorneys. It can happen anywhere in the world.

Not So Happy Birthday

Birth certificates are documents that can be used to establish phony identities. This makes them a valuable commodity, or at least that is what Jose M. Aponte thought when he tried to sell more than 1,000 blank birth certificates to an undercover FBI agent, who apparently

364.1633 LEV

16	
17	
22	
23	

18 - Wed	Book Discussion: The Summer Before the War - 3 pm
19 - Thu	Getting Fiscally Fit - 7 pm
20 - Fri	Friday Night Movie: Sully - 7 pm
24 - Tue	Book Discussion: Still Life - 7 pm

already had an identity. Aponte was asking for $225,000, but what he wound up getting was a sentence of two years and three months in federal prison.

It Can Happen to Anyone

United States Senator Pete Domenici from New Mexico lost his wallet in Albuquerque in March 2004. When his next credit card statement arrived, he learned that identity theft even strikes United States senators. His credit card had been used for a criminal shopping spree.

It's Not Nice to Fool with Mother Nature

A popular television advertising campaign in 1971 for Chiffon margarine featured an angry Mother Nature wreaking havoc on someone who substituted Chiffon margarine for natural butter. Before inflicting her wrath, she proclaimed, "It's not nice to fool Mother Nature." Similarly, it is not nice, and probably not too smart either, to steal the identity of a district attorney. However, that is just what was done to Harris County Texas District Attorney Chuck Rosenthal, whose checking account was accessed by an identity thief who managed to steal close to $8,000 from the account before being caught. With resources the average identity thief victim might not have quite so readily available, one of the checks used by the identity thief to steal the money was analyzed, and provided a fingerprint. Criminal charges soon followed. It's not nice to fool with a District Attorney.

Belgian Waffling

In March 2004, Belgian police investigators uncovered the biggest identity theft ring in Belgian history. Police were first alerted to the fact that something was awry when a number of stores that sold expensive electronic products in Brussels and another Belgian city experienced unusually high sales volume. Further investigation uncovered the fact that a large amount of these goods were sold to Southeast Asians who used credit cards from all over the world. It later turned out that the credit cards were forgeries and that the people using them were members of a Southeast Asian crime gang that had obtained a database of legitimate credit card numbers from a Russian organized crime group. The Russian group had hacked its way into the computerized billing system of a major international hotel chain, stealing the credit card information that was then used to create forged credit cards. These cards were later traced to fraudulent purchases in Germany, France, the Netherlands, and Germany.

Battling the Companies with Which You Do Business

It is certainly disheartening to be a victim of identity theft, but having to battle with the companies with which you regularly do business following the discovery of your identity being compromised is almost beyond comprehension.

Twice Victimized

It's bad enough being the victim of identity theft, but add to that being victimized by your own finance company and you have a problem that could have been the subject of a Kafka novel, had identity theft existed in his time.

Robert Korinke and his wife attempted to take advantage of lower mortgage interest rates by refinancing their home in 2001. That is when they first learned of $75,000 of debt appearing on their credit reports as a result of identity theft. Apparently an identity thief had accessed an equity credit line they had on their home and run up this substantial amount of debt. The Korinkes were particularly taken by surprise because the equity credit line that had been compromised was one they had already closed. The identity thief not only had managed to get a hold of their equity credit line account, but he arranged for the address of the account to be changed so that as he ran up his debt, the Korinkes remained unaware. It took a few months, but eventually the Korinkes were able to convince Homecomings Financial Network, Inc., the issuer of the equity credit line, that they had not authorized the use of the equity credit line by the identity thief and not to hold them responsible for the debt. Or so they thought. Two years later, as an early Christmas present on December 23, 2003, they were served with a civil complaint informing them that they were being sued by Homecomings not only for the $75,000 of debt run up by the identity thief, but for Homecomings's attorneys fees as well. In other words, they were being sued for the unauthorized charges as well as Homecomings's costs in suing them.

An unusual aspect of this case was that the lawsuit alleged that the Korinkes had been negligent due to their delay in finding out about and reporting the identity thievery. The Korinkes lawyer convinced Homecomings, in relatively short order, to drop the lawsuit, but a new twist had been added to the problems of identity theft: institutions looking toward the victims of identity theft for compensation for losses the institutions may have suffered.

"The Same Old Watson! You Never Learn That the Gravest Issues May Depend Upon the Smallest Things."

This quote comes from Sherlock Holmes in *The Adventures of the Creeping Man*. It also may describe the unfortunate misadventures of another John Watson of more recent ilk. In 2003, John Watson first learned that he had been a victim of identity theft when he noticed that $7,600 had been taken from his Bank of America bank account. After a Holmesian investigation, he learned that an identity thief had opened a PayPal account in Watson's name and was able to get at money from Watson's bank account to pay for purchases using PayPal. You would think that after this became apparent, Watson would be in the clear. However, John Watson, like the Korinkes, was in for an expensive lesson. Although the money had been taken from his account during the summer of 2002, Watson did not first learn of the money being missing from his Bank of America account until January 2003 because he had been traveling extensively out of town. Watson's problem was compounded by the fact that, unlike credit card laws pertaining to responsibility for unauthorized use, the laws governing electronic transfers do not provide as much protection. As I indicated earlier, with an electronic transfer, if you notify the institution within two days that your account has been accessed improperly, your liability is limited to $50 If your report of the theft is made between three and sixty days after the theft, your responsibility for unauthorized charges is limited to $500. But if your report of unauthorized use is made more than sixty days after the theft occurs, the law has no limit to your financial responsibility. Yikes! This problem can be particularly troublesome with identity theft because most victims of identity theft do not learn that they are victims until long after the theft has occurred.

PayPal and Watson's other pal, Bank of America were not terribly cooperative with John Watson over this matter, or perhaps that is exactly what they were—terribly cooperative. With some effort, Watson was able to convince PayPal to return to Watson the $2,100 that remained in the fraudulent PayPal account that had been set up in Watson's name by the identity thief who had victimized him. But this still left John Watson $5,500 in the hole. When negotiating and pleading with both Bank of America and PayPal went nowhere, Watson took his case to the bargain basement of the law—small claims court. He sued both Bank of America and PayPal for his remaining loss of $5,500. Acting as his own attorney, he argued that despite the laws regarding electronic transactions, PayPal was negligent in not notifying him more promptly that a fraud had occurred. A sympathetic judge ruled in John Watson's favor. The tale has a bittersweet ending. Because the limit on a small claims court action was $5,000, the checks John Watson received from Bank of America and PayPal were limited to $2,500 from each. He ended up forfeiting $500. Still, all in all, John Watson handled himself in a way that would have made Sherlock Holmes proud.

Can't I Sue Somebody?

P. Kenneth Huggins was the victim of an identity thief who used Huggins' identity to obtain credit cards and get cash and merchandise without ever paying for anything. In a new approach to this problem, P. Kenneth Huggins sued three banks—Citibank, Capital One Bank, and Premier Bankcard—that had issued credit cards to the identity thief arguing that their negligent actions enabled the identity thief to commit his crime. In his complaint, Huggins alleged that the banks issued the cards "with no investigation, no verification, no identification, no corroboration, and no effort whatever to determine whether Doe (the identity thief was referred to as 'John Doe' in the complaint) was who he claimed to be." The case went to the South Carolina Supreme Court, where in 2003 the court ruled in favor of the banks saying that on technical grounds the bank did not owe any duty of care to P. Kenneth Huggins because Huggins was not a customer of the banks. The case hinged on this legal technicality because, as Justice E.C. Burnett III who wrote the decision of the South Carolina Supreme Court in this case indicated on behalf of the court, "Even though it is foreseeable that injury might arise by the negligent issuance of a credit card, foreseeability alone does not give rise to a duty."

✤ Have I Got a Deal For You

Cocktail chatter in recent years has often revolved around who obtained the lowest mortgage rate for their refinancing. Fully aware of this, identity thieves pose as mortgage brokers who will provide access to an incredibly low rate after the sucker, I mean applicant, provides personal financial information. The point is, as always; make sure you know with whom you are dealing and that they are legitimate.

And for Dessert, Your Credit Card

A skimmer is the name for a small electronic device, about the size of a credit card that is operated by a waiter with a larcenous heart who, when he takes your credit card at the end of a satisfying meal, runs your card not only through normal processing, but also quickly swipes it through the skimmer which gathers all the personal information contained on the card. Identity thieves pay conspiring waiters a bounty for each card from which they steal the information necessary to steal your identity. The solution: If possible, observe your card whenever it is outside of your possession. The reality of the situation is, however, that this is a difficult rule to follow.

Endnotes

1. Remsburg v. Docusearch, Inc. New Hampshire Supreme Court no. 2003-255.

6

TECHNOLOGY, BUSINESS, AND GOVERNMENT FIGHT IDENTITY THEFT

he low-cost availability of computer technology has made the work of identity thieves extremely easy. It seems only fair that technology may also hold the keys to winning the battle against identity theft.

High Tech Tactics to Combat Identity Theft

Biometrics

The term "biometrics" is derived from Latin, meaning "life measurement," and it shows great promise in the battle against identity theft. The Fair and Accurate Credit Transactions Act of 2003 (FACT) even contains a provision requiring the Federal Trade Commission to study whether biometrics and other technological advances can be used to fight identity theft. Various biometric technologies that are being tested and used now include fingerprinting, earprinting, retina scanning, iris scanning, voice recognition, facial recognition, handwriting analysis, hand print recognition, and hand vein geometry.

At the heart of any effective biometric system is not just some sort of measurement of a unique physical characteristic of a person, but also the confirmation of that person's identity through comparison of those measurements with a readily accessible computer databank of the measurements of the general population. The most famous existing database is the FBI's Integrated Automated Fingerprint Identification System (IAFIS), which is capable of performing more than 100,000 comparisons per second—in 15 minutes it can complete a data bank review of more than 42 million records.

No system is perfect. In constructing any system there is always a delicate balance between the rates of false acceptances and false rejections. False acceptances occur when a person is wrongfully matched to someone else's biometric measurement maintained in the central data bank. False rejections occur when a person's biometric measurement fails to be matched with his biometric measurement maintained in the central databank. Generally, manipulating the system to lessen false acceptances tends to increase the rate of false rejections, while adjusting the system to reduce false rejection causes an increase in the rate of false acceptances. In the real world, no system is perfect. When security concerns are highest, systems tilted toward minimizing false acceptances are usually used. When such a system is used, however, it is necessary to have a backup procedure for establishing the identity of someone who has been wrongfully rejected by the system.

A major security concern that should be addressed by any biometric identification system is to ensure that the database is protected from hackers gaining access to the central database system and switching or altering data.

Garbage In—Garbage Out

An old computer axiom is "garbage in—garbage out," which means that when invalid data is entered into a computer system, the resulting output will also be invalid regardless of how good the system itself is. Whatever biometric system is used, a crucial moment for establishing the reliability of the system is the establishment of the database to which future measurements will be compared. An identity thief who can compromise that initial step by, for instance, using a stolen Social Security number or a phony birth certificate in order to have his own biometric measurements assigned to someone else's identity, is at a tremendous advantage in utilizing identity theft for fraudulent purposes. Another opportunity for an identity thief to manipulate a biometric system is by having his measurements entered into the system as belonging to a number of different identities that he would utilize for criminal purposes.

Privacy Concerns

Privacy advocates are particularly concerned about whether the vast collection of identifying data necessary for an effective biometric system is worth the invasion of people's privacy and whether the system could be too easily misused to monitor the population by both government and businesses. It is a legitimate concern and one that must be dealt with in any discussion of the use of biometrics.

Oh, Grandma, What Big Ears You Have

Little Red Riding Hood may have been one of the pioneers when it came to using ear recognition as a biometric technique. However, researchers at the University of Leicester in the United Kingdom have taken that technique a bit farther, having developed a computerized system based on what they say are unique shapes and features of people's ears. The computerized system compares 14 to 18 specific places on the ear and matches them to a database of ear measurements. Until this system was in place, earprints were matched manually at an obviously much slower pace. As odd as earprints may seem to us, earprinting identification actually predates fingerprinting. In recent years, earprinting has been used in criminal investigations in the United Kingdom, the Netherlands and Switzerland.

Earprinting has its critics, though. Australian law enforcement personnel have been particularly critical of its reliability. In a particularly noteworthy case, a 2004 U.K. murder conviction was overturned on the grounds that the earprint comparison used to connect the defendant to the crime was too subjective. Eventually, conclusive DNA evidence exonerated the defendant and brought into question the effectiveness of the earprinting technique.

Voice Recognition

Voice recognition has the benefit of simplicity and being a non-invasive technology. Its drawbacks are that voices change over time and are subject to manipulation by a clever identity thief. Comedian-impressionist Rich Little would have a field day if he ever turned to the dark side of the force. In addition, there is the problem of a voice recognition system being manipulated by an identity thief with a tape recording of the voice of his victim.

The Future Is Now

Bank United of Texas has been using iris recognition instead of PIN numbers at its ATMs since 2000, and the reaction of consumers has been generally quite positive. Quite eye-opening. Unfortunately, for me iris recognition always brings back disgusting thoughts of Tom Cruise as Detective John Anderton undergoing a double eyeball transplant in the movie *Minority Report* in order to gain access to a building that uses iris scanning for identification purposes. The technology behind iris scanning recognition is of fairly recent origin. Iris scanning is not only highly accurate, but also is a system that is relatively simple to operate. A video camera scans a person's eye from around twenty inches away and takes a picture of the iris, that is considered to be unique. Problems can occur, however, if the person's iris is dilated due to drug use or if colored contact lenses are worn. An advantage of iris scanning is that a reading can be compared to a database of iris records significantly faster than fingerprints due to fewer items within the scan having to be matched.

Ophthalmologist Frank Burch first proposed the use of iris patterns for personal identification as far back as 1936, but it was not until 1987 that ophthalmologists Aran Safir and Leonard Flom patented the idea. Algorithms created by Cambridge University Professor John Daugman led to his creation of software that provides for the analysis of the multifaceted image of the iris.

When it comes to beating the system, criminals who are Tom Cruise fans would not be able to cut out someone's eye and hold it up to the camera to manipulate the test. According to Professor Daugman, when the eye is removed from the body the pupil dilates significantly and the cornea turns cloudy, making this attempt to fool the system worthless.

Presently iris scans are already starting to make inroads in criminal identification. The Barnstable County Massachusetts jail was one of the early users of this technology.

Retinal Scans

Of the new biometric identity techniques, retinal scans are probably the most accurate but far from the simplest for establishing an all-important initial database. Retinal scans measure the unique pattern of blood vessels in the eye. Retinal patterns generally remain constant during a person's entire life;

however, diseases of the eye such as glaucoma or cataracts can change a person's retinal pattern. Unfortunately, at present the process for performing a retinal scan is time consuming and cumbersome, requiring the subject to keep his or her head still, focusing an eye on a specific location while an infrared beam is applied through the pupil of the eye. The reflected light is then measured and recorded by a camera.

Fingerprints

One of the oldest and still most dependable forms of biometrics is fingerprinting. It is a tried-and-true identification system that is already in place, highly accurate, and cost effective. But it is not perfect. The highly sophisticated FBI IAFIS still has a two to three percent false rejection rate. A number of states—California, Texas, Colorado, Oklahoma, Hawaii, and Georgia—already require drivers to provide a fingerprint when they get driver's licenses or renew their licenses. The state of Washington has a voluntary system allowing fingerprints, retinal scans, and other biometric measures to be used when obtaining or replacing a driver's license.

Systems also already exist that could be used for fingerprint confirmation when applying for a driver's license, through which a person's finger would be placed on a scanner that would transmit the data to a main computer and compare the print to prints contained within its database. A match would bring up a photograph of the person that could be transmitted back to the Department of Motor Vehicles. If the picture matched the person applying for or renewing a license, the license would be issued. If it did not match, further inquiry would occur. The new driver's license issued using this procedure would carry a magnetic strip such as is found on credit cards. In this case, the strip would contain a digital encryption of the fingerprint that could be used for future identity confirmation. One fly in this ointment is that if the information contained in the original database was tainted or compromised by an identity thief, anything flowing from that would be further corrupted.

Providing a new meaning to giving the finger to the check out clerk, the Piggly Wiggly stores in some states already utilize a Pay by Touch system by which you place your finger on a scanner at the check-out counter to purchase groceries. The scanner measures 40 specific data points on your finger that are encrypted into a unique mathematical equation to identify you and also access your bank account.

Unfortunately, the very fact that fingerprinting has been with us so long also means that criminals have had many years in which to develop ways to beat that system. Applying glue to fingers before being fingerprinted can cover the skin ridges that make up a fingerprint, rendering it useless as an identifier. Common household cleaners can even be used to change ridges on the finger necessary for a readable fingerprint. Fingerprint readings may also be affected by dirt on the fingertips or the condition of the skin. Finally, both the taking of initial fingerprints and the matching process are activities that require a significant level of skill to be done correctly.

₂ Look at That Face

Facial recognition is another non-invasive technology that is still in its infancy, but offers some promise. Some Internet banks are testing facial recognition systems that would use Web cameras to confirm the identity of bank customers seeking access to their accounts through their computers over the Internet. Unfortunately, tests done by the Defense Department and the International Biometric Group, a research and consulting firm concluded that using present technology, correct matches are accomplished only about 54% of the time.[1] Facial recognition also has the drawbacks of being subject to too many sources of error, including effects of light, facial expression, and weight gain.

₂ Brotherly Love

James Dalton of Xenia, Ohio was sentenced to jail for three years in his own name after being convicted of stealing his brother's name. It was a relatively easy thing for Dalton to obtain his brother's name, birth date, and Social Security number while his brother was serving in the military in the Middle East. Armed with this information, Dalton got a credit card in his brother's name and went on a shopping spree that ultimately landed him in jail.

⁑ Car Thieves Who Don't Steal Cars

Many car thieves are less interested in your car than the contents of it. Your cash is an easy target, but so are your credit cards, checkbooks, and any other material that can translate into identity theft.

Eric Ziegler was convicted in 2004 of multiple charges involving break-ins to cars. Ziegler stole checks, credit cards, and identification cards from the purses of women whom he observed leaving their cars without their purses.

Tip *Lock your car and don't leave anything in it that you cannot risk losing.*

⁑ I'm Paul Casey

This is an era of specialization. Apparently identity thief David Faulcon specialized in identity theft from people named Paul Casey, at least 12 of them in Massachusetts. The apparent source of the information used to steal the identities of Paul Caseys throughout Massachusetts was the Massachusetts Registry of Motor Vehicles. One of the victimized Paul Caseys was Massachusetts state legislator Paul C. Casey, who has understandably become a strong advocate for more comprehensive identity theft laws.

✎ Some Day My Prince Will Come (Back)

On February 19, 2004 Prince Christian Okolie, a Nigerian living in Dallas, Texas was convicted on five counts of identity theft crimes. The maximum sentence for his crimes was 40 years in prison and a 1.25 million-dollar fine. You might wonder what Prince Christian Okolie's reaction was to being found guilty of his crimes and facing such a devastating potential penalty. If so, you will have to keep wondering because when the jury came back with guilty verdicts, Prince Christian Okolie had left the courtroom during a break in the trial after telling his lawyer that he needed to make a telephone call. He never returned. Federal law permits a trial to continue when a defendant is voluntarily absent, so the trial proceeded for one more day until its completion.

Okolie's pattern of identity theft was a familiar one. He used personal information from unwary victims to open bank accounts into which he would deposit checks that he had stolen and altered to reflect the name of the person whose identity he had stolen. After the checks cleared, he withdrew the money. As is so often the case with identity theft, a number of his victims testified during the trial that they had no idea how he obtained their personal information.

Three Million Credit Cards

How many credit cards do you have? Chances are, no matter how many you have, you do not have more than James M. Lyle, a young man who at the tender age of 19 pleaded guilty to using counterfeit credit cards after Pittsburgh police officers found more than three million phony credit card numbers on his computer. A computer program, which generated the numbers in the summer of 2003, enabled Lyle to make fraudulent purchases over the Internet. Following his conviction, he was sentenced to 27 months in federal prison.

Business Fights Back

Business often is accused of not doing enough to reduce or stop identity theft. Some people believe businesses consider it a cost of business that businesses just pass on to their customers. However, The Financial Services Roundtable, an organization of 100 of the largest financial service companies from banking to insurance to investments has created a pilot project called the Identity Theft Assistance Center to help combat identity theft. Victims of identity theft can make a single telephone to their local bank that takes over from there and brings the Identity Theft Assistance Center into action. The Identity Theft Assistance Center contacts the identity theft victim and coordinates the drafting of an identity theft affidavit to be provided to law enforcement agencies, credit card companies, the credit reporting bureaus, and other companies with which the victim does business. The Identity Theft Assistance Center also maintains a secure database of the names of identity theft victims. The database is available to financial institutions receiving credit or loan applications so that they can easily determine whether the name of the person requesting a loan or credit is the same as someone who has been reported as being the victim of identity theft.

Identity Theft Insurance

From high technology biometrics to low technology identity theft insurance, the recognition by businesses and government that identity theft is a problem that must be dealt with in as many ways possible is a good development.

In response to the problems presented by identity theft in recent years, the financial industry has developed identity theft insurance. Generally, these policies are not used to reimburse you for money that may have been stolen from you through identity theft. Instead, they will help pay for the costs involved with correcting the problems that come with identity theft, such as fixing your credit report and lost wages due to taking time off from work due to the time and burden involved in repairing your credit.

Some homeowners' or renters' insurance policies provide as much as $25,000 of coverage for identity theft for little or no additional cost. A number of major insurance companies also offer separate identity theft policies for relatively small annual premiums of between $25 and $195. Finally, many credit cards offer identity theft protection as an optional benefit for cardholders, some at no cost. Some card issuers provide the insurance to all their credit card customers, whereas others provide it as either an additional benefit of their premium cards or as an inducement to new customers to apply for the particular card providing this benefit.

But regardless of how little the premium might be, do you really need the coverage? Generally, you are not responsible for unauthorized charges beyond $50, and most companies do not even hold you responsible for that amount. The real cost of identity theft for many people is the cost of the time it takes to have their good name and their good credit restored. If you do opt for an identity theft insurance policy, look for one with a low deductible and one that will provide for payment of legal fees, which can be considerable if an identity thief commits crimes in your name.

Culture of Security

"Culture of Security" sounds like it might relate to the 1980's band "Culture Club" led by Boy George. However, in fact it is the name given to the goal of the Federal Trade Commission (FTC) to safeguard information security, particularly online. The FTC is active in both domestic and international cybersecurity initiatives. In early 2004, the FTC began promoting "Operation Secure Your Server," a joint effort with 36 agencies from 26 other countries to reduce spam on a worldwide basis. In addition, the FTC works on information security issues with the Asian Pacific Economic Cooperation forum, the United Nations, the TransAtlantic Business and Consumer Dialogues, the Global Business Dialogue on Electronic Commerce, and others.

Just Do the Best You Can

When I was a teacher at Old Colony Correctional Institution (a fancy name for one of the Massachusetts state prisons), one of my students was serving two consecutive life sentences. I asked him about that apparent contradiction. After all, how can you serve two life sentences? He first explained to me that he had the same thought at the time of his sentencing and with apparent irritation in his voice had asked how the judge expected him to serve two life sentences, to which the judge responded, "Just do the best you can." My student later told me that the real reason for being sentenced to two life sentences was that if his appeal was successful on one of the crimes for which he was sentenced to life in prison, the state would still have the other sentence hanging over him.

I tell you that story because, unfortunately, with so much of your personal information found in the records of your employer, your accountant, your lawyer, your doctor, your health insurer, your bank, and so on and so on, we are all vulnerable to a bad apple working in one of those offices. Identity theft can be as high tech as a hacker breaking into a company's computer system from afar and stealing personal information or as low tech as an identity thief going through your trash. The best you can do is to try to minimize your vulnerability and be vigilant and ready to respond if you discover a breach of security.

Endnotes

1. Jonathon Phillips et al, An Introduction to Evaluating Biometric Systems, Computer [2000], http://www.dodcounterrug.com/facialrecognition/DLs/Feret7.pdf

7

FINANCIAL PRIVACY PLEASE: THE GRAMM-LEACH-BLILEY ACT

T he privacy of your personal financial information held by companies with which you do business is not just a matter of an increase in junk mail solicitations from such companies. The less private and secure your personal financial information is, the more likely you are to be a victim of identity theft.

Which appears more difficult to remember: the Gramm-Leach-Bliley Act or the Financial Services Modernization Act? Whatever you call it, when it comes to protecting the privacy of consumers, the law is a confusing amalgam of guidelines that help the financial industries much more than they do consumers. Although trumpeted by some politicians as a law that helps to protect consumers' privacy, the Gramm-Leach-Bliley Act, a federal law, does little to achieve that end. Rather, its intention all along was to legalize banks', insurance companies', and investment companies' ability to merge or more effectively do business together.

The four main parts of the Gramm-Leach-Bliley Act that directly apply to consumers deal with disclosure of companies' privacy policies; opting out of providing information to non-affiliated third parties; non-disclosure of personal account information, and setting standards to protect security and confidentiality of consumers' private information.

You might remember receiving the first annual disclosure of the privacy policies of the financial companies with which you do business, such as banks, insurance companies, credit card companies, and brokerage companies. Or then again, maybe you don't because many of us just looked at these disclosures and considered them to be just more pieces of junk mail from our banks or credit card companies. Few of us took a moment to actually try to read them and those that did often found them indecipherable. In any event, just like the swallows returning to Capistrano or your relatives returning for Thanksgiving, these disclosures are required by law to be sent to you every year.

The privacy disclosure is required by law to be a clear, conspicuous, and accurate statement of the particular company's information sharing and privacy policy. Unfortunately, the disclosures are generally unclear and inconspicuous. They are an all too accurate statement of the consumer's lack of control over his or her personal financial information. The disclosure must describe the particular institution's policy in regard to the personal "experience and transaction information" that it collects, as well as the company's policy for disclosure of non-public personal information to both third parties and companies affiliated with the particular institution. Experience and transaction information consists of extraordinarily personal information such as your bank account number, how much money you have in your bank account, what you have purchased with your credit cards, how much life insurance you have, and your Social Security number. It even includes information that you may have provided to the company without even knowing that you had done so through the placement of "cookies" in your computer by a company with which you have done business online. In the world of computers, cookies are pieces of text that permit a website to store information on your computer's hard drive and then retrieve it later without you being aware that the process is occurring. Through the use of cookies, a company operating a website you visit is able to trace everywhere you have gone on the Internet. If you want to see what particular cookies are on your computer, you can go to c:\windows\cookies. This applies to most PCs. You also can delete cookies from your computer if you want to.

Prior to the enactment of the Gramm-Leach-Bliley Act and unbeknownst to many consumers, financial institutions such as banks and brokerage houses had been sharing consumers' personal experience and transaction information not just with companies with which they already were affiliated in some fashion, but with telemarketers as well. The Gramm-Leach-Bliley Act still permits these financial institutions to share this sensitive information with affiliated companies, even if you request that they not do so. An affiliated company is one that is either owned or controlled by the company with which you do business. The Gramm-Leach-Bliley Act also permits financial institutions to share your personal information with other companies that have joint marketing agreements with the company with which you are doing business. An example of a joint marketing agreement is a program by which your bank agrees to endorse or offer insurance policies issued by another company. As a bone thrown to consumers, the law now prohibits the sharing of this information with telemarketers. By the way, if you have not yet signed up for the National Do Not Call List to stop annoying calls from telemarketers, you may wish to do so. You can register for the list, which is operated by the Federal Trade Commission, by going to their website at www.donotcall.gov or by calling them at 1-888-382-1222. The process is quick, easy, and rewarding.

Perhaps most importantly to consumers, the disclosure must also provide consumers with a way to exercise the right to opt out of the sharing of non-public personal information with non-affiliated companies.

Some sharing of information is allowed regardless of whether you choose to opt out, and in some instances this rule makes sense. Private information may be shared with third parties necessary to service your account, with credit reporting agencies, and to comply with investigations by state and federal regulatory agencies. In other instances, your information is shared with companies because they are affiliated in some way with the company with which you are doing business, regardless of whether you have chosen to opt out of information sharing. These situations exemplify the consumer's weakness and the strength of the lobbying of the financial industries.

Rubbing salt in the wounds, some financial institution executives have even had the gall to suggest that the reason so few people have chosen to opt out of information sharing is that consumers appreciate the "benefits" of having their personal information shared with other companies. Those so-called "benefits" include having your privacy compromised and becoming more susceptible to identity theft. The truth of the matter is that the reason relatively few people have exercised their limited power to opt out of information sharing is that either they did not understand the disclosure form sent to them or they just threw it away, considering it to be merely junk mail.

One of the better provisions of the Gramm-Leach-Bliley Act is its prohibition from sharing account numbers or other identifying numbers with non-affiliated telemarketers, direct mail marketers, or e-mail marketers.

Safeguard Rules

In an attempt to provide for better security and privacy of personal information, the Gramm-Leach-Bliley Act also requires financial institutions to set up new standards to protect the confidentiality and security of consumers' personal information to help aid in the battle against identity theft and fraud. Under the safeguard rules provisions of the Gramm-Leach-Bliley Act, every company that is "significantly engaged" in providing financial services or products to consumers must develop a written plan to secure the privacy of personal customer information. This section of the law applies not only to banks, brokerage houses, and insurance companies, but also credit reporting agencies, mortgage brokers, real estate appraisers, tax preparers, and even ordinary retailers that issue their own store credit cards. Specifically, the plan must note and assess the risks to consumers' personal information throughout each aspect of the company's activities. The company's present security systems must be evaluated and regularly updated to respond to changes inside and outside of the company.

Due to the fact that a company's employees with access to sensitive, personal information are an always present possible source of identity theft, companies are urged to pay particular attention to the references of employees being hired who will have access to such information. A proper safeguard plan also provides rules for locking areas and file cabinets where written records are stored, establishing and regularly changing computer passwords, and encrypting personal consumer information whenever possible.

Pretexting

The Gramm-Leach-Bliley Act also makes "pretexting" illegal. Pretexting is the term for the fraudulent obtaining of consumers' personal financial information by the use of false pretenses. Pretexting comes in many variations, such as someone pretending to be taking a survey or pretending through a website to be a financial institution with which you do business requesting confirmation of personal financial information, which when provided starts you on the road to identity theft.

Opt Out, Opt In

In the movie *The Karate Kid*, Mr. Miyagi's mantra was "Wax on, Wax off." This was the mundane way that he taught young Daniel to protect himself. If you don't know what I'm talking about, go rent the video. You will enjoy it. In the world of the security of your personal financial information, the mantra is "Opt in, Opt out." When the comprehensive Financial Services Modernization Act was being debated in Congress, the issue of whether consumers should be required to affirmatively opt out of having their personal information shared or whether they should be required to opt in if they wanted their personal information shared was hotly debated. Ultimately the final score on this matter was Big Bad Financial Institutions 2 (I guess you know where I stand), Consumers 0. Not only did Congress drastically limit the circumstances in which we could prevent the sharing of our personal information, but it also, in the ultimate caving-in to the Big Bad Financial Institutions, required us to take affirmative steps to prevent the sharing of our personal information. So much for a government of the people, by the people, and for the people. But let's look at this dirty glass as half-full instead of half-empty and consider how you can opt out of information sharing. If you have neglected to take this step and opt out in order to protect yourself from identity theft and reduce the amount of annoying marketing junk mail you receive, you can still exercise your limited right to opt out of information sharing by sending a letter to the various financial institutions with which you deal requesting that they not share your personal information. A copy of a form letter to opt out is included in Chapter 15, "Form Letters." Generally, the disclosure that you receive from the financial companies with which you do business allows you to exercise your limited right to opt out of information sharing either through a letter or form sent back to them, by way of a toll-free telephone call, or through the Internet, if that is how you normally do business with that particular company.

Good Guys in Congress

There are some good guys from both parties in Congress trying to protect consumers' rights, and although they did not win the war when it came to the Gramm-Leach-Bliley Act, they did win some battles. Democratic Senator Paul Sarbanes was able to add an amendment to the bill while it was being considered that at least allowed the individual states to enact their own stronger laws to protect the privacy of personal information held by financial institutions. North Dakota passed such a law, which serves as a model to other states so inclined to provide greater privacy protection to their citizens.

The Bottom Line

The plain, hard fact is that the more places that have personal information about you, the more risk of identity theft you face. Much identity theft originates with criminal employees of legitimate companies stealing information to which they have ready access. And it just stands to reason that the more places your information is found, the more places exist for identity thieves to find it. Whether these identity thieves are company employees or hackers from outside the company makes little difference to you. The result is the same. Your identity is stolen. But you can reduce your chances of becoming the victim of identity theft by merely "opting out," telling the Big Bad Financial Institutions that at least to the fullest extent that the law permits, you do not want them to share your information with anyone. The Big Bad Financial Institutions that have your information depend on all of us being too lazy to read the interminably boring, small-printed notices they send us that tell us about our rights to opt out of information sharing. They do not want us to be the victims of identity theft, but they do want to use and disseminate this information for business and marketing purposes. And when it comes to protecting our privacy or increasing their business, which do you think is their priority? So opt out. Opt out now. Okay, you can wait until you finish the book, but then opt out; go directly to opt out. Do not pass go. Do not collect $200. Go directly to opt out.

8

CREDIT CARDS

C redit cards are a necessity of modern day life. Have you ever tried to rent a car without a credit card? Unfortunately, choosing the right credit card is a task that is fraught with peril. However, the more you know about credit cards and how they work, the better your chances of finding a credit card best suited for you and your spending habits.

The History of Credit

Credit goes back to ancient Egypt more than 3,000 years ago (and if they had had credit cards back then, someone using them paying the minimum on a credit card might still be paying off his or her purchases). The first charge cards were department store cards that appeared around 1914. They were limited to purchases of the card issuer's goods and services.

Plastic Man

Although it may seem like credit cards have been with us forever, it was not until 1950 that Diners Club issued the first credit card that was originally used at, not surprisingly, restaurants. The "Aha!" moment that spurred the creation of Diners Club occurred when Frank X. McNamara joined his lawyer Ralph Sneider and his friend Alfred Bloomingdale (yes, of those Bloomingdales) for dinner on an evening in 1949 at the Major's Cabin Grill, a New York City restaurant. When McNamara reached for his wallet to retrieve some cash to pay for the meal, he suddenly realized that he had neglected to bring his wallet. Oops! A telephone call to his wife remedied the situation and she brought him the necessary money. But, taking a bad situation and turning it into a good and profitable one, the incident inspired McNamara to come up with the idea of a credit card that could be used at many different places rather than just at one store, as was the custom of the time. McNamara brought his idea to the two friends with whom he had that insightful dinner and a new company was born—Diners Club. As McNamara envisioned it, Diners Club would be the facilitator for the providing of credit through businesses by offering credit to individuals on behalf of these businesses. Diners Club would then bill the individuals, collect the money, and pay the businesses. A business model was born, and the three men formed Diners Club. Interest was not charged, and payment in full was required each month. The source of the profit for Diners Club was the combination of a small annual fee to card holders beginning at $3 in 1951 and a 7 percent surcharge to the merchants subscribing to Diners Club on each purchase.

In keeping with the name, the first businesses that accepted Diners Club cards were 14 New York restaurants. And although we talk about credit cards as "plastic," the first Diners Club card, as odd as it may seem today, was printed on paper. From an initial distribution of 200 Diners Club cards, membership soared to 20,000 in the first year. Within two years, the company had turned a profit, and the visionary Frank McNamara sold his interest in Diners Club to Sneider and Bloomingdale for $200,000 because he was convinced that credit cards were just a fad.

Don't Leave Home Without It

About eight years after the Diners Club experiment, American Express decided people should not leave home without one of their cards and they joined the credit card business. To be perfectly clear (as Richard Nixon used to say), their card is not a credit card, but rather, like the first department store cards and the Diners Club cards, a charge card because the amount you charge on an American Express card must be paid in full each month.

Credit cards became increasingly popular with the advent of the bank credit card system that we now know as MasterCard and Visa. Visa, which in 1959 was called BankAmericard, was the first national bank credit card company to set up a system by which the individual banks involved credited the accounts of merchants with whom they had accounts when BankAmericard received the sales receipts. The banks that made up BankAmericard paid the stores immediately. At the end of the billing period, the cardholder received a monthly statement from BankAmericard showing all his or her charges and had the option to either pay the entire account in full or pay a required minimum along with interest on the unpaid balance. Master Charge, which later changed its name to MasterCard, soon began following suit, and an American way of life was born.

Very Interesting

Comic actor Arte Johnson used to play a character on the television show, *Rowan and Martin's Laugh-In* who had a line that became part of the lexicon: "Very Interesting." When credit cards first became part of the national landscape, they were not that interesting to the credit card companies. Each state had its own usury laws that limited the amount of interest that could be charged on credit cards provided to people within that state, and many of these states' interest rates were relatively low. The 1978 Supreme Court case of Marquette National Bank of Minneapolis vs. First Omaha Service Corp. changed things. This case involved the solicitation of Minnesota credit card customers by First Omaha, a Nebraska bank that was trying to use the higher interest rates allowed by Nebraska law rather than the low (at the time) 8 percent interest limit provided for by Minnesota law. In a landmark decision, the Supreme Court ruled that credit card issuers would be able to charge their out-of-state customers the highest interest rate permitted in the bank's home state.

The Marquette decision ushered in a new era in credit card expansion, with some states seeing this as an opportunity to attract banking business through the lifting of interest limiting usury laws.

Trivia That Can Win You a Bar Bet

Have you ever wondered what the numbers on your credit card mean? Neither have I, which is why if you are ever looking to win some easy money in a bar bet, you might tell someone that you can guess the first digit on their

MasterCard credit card. The answer is 5. The answer is always 5, just as the answer is always 4 for Visa, 6 for Discover, and 3 for American Express. As a matter of fact, the second digit on an American Express card is always 7. On a MasterCard and Visa, the remaining numbers signify the bank number and the account number.

Tip   *Always sign your card as soon as you get it. Although many clerks do not even bother to check your signature when you make a purchase, it still is a good way to keep your card secure.*

Do not give your credit card number over the telephone to anyone unless you have placed the call and you are sure to whom you are speaking.

Don't forget to get your card back when you make a purchase. A good way to remember to do this is to keep your wallet or credit card holder out until your credit card is returned. And then immediately put it back into your wallet.

Maintain a list of all of your credit card numbers and the toll free numbers to call if your card is lost or stolen.

Fees

According to the old saying, "There is no free lunch." I do not know if this necessarily implies that breakfast and dinner are up for grabs, but there certainly are no free credit cards. Increased fees on credit cards now account for 35 percent of the income of credit card companies as compared with about 18 percent ten years ago. Some of the common fees are detailed in the following paragraphs.

Annual Fee

An annual fee is a yearly charge for the privilege of doing business with the credit card company. The amounts can vary considerably from card to card. Fortunately, according to cardweb.com, only about 20 percent of bank credit cards come with an annual fee. And many of those that do charge an annual fee will waive your fee if you are a good customer. The amount of green that you have to pay for the annual fee for your card is often dependent upon the color of your card, with gold cards more costly than regular cards and platinum cards more costly than gold cards. The gold standard has sunk considerably in recent years, and it is important to see just what you are getting for the extra money—other than a colorful card—because there are many gold cards that are only offering you phony prestige without significant benefits tied to the card's color.

Minimum Finance Charge

With fewer and fewer credit card companies charging annual fees, more and more credit card companies are now charging minimum monthly finance fees of between two and six dollars, regardless of whether you pay your account in full each month. In other words, it is just an annual fee in disguise except you now pay monthly for the privilege of having a particular credit card. If it walks like a duck, looks like a duck, and quacks like a duck, it's a duck. And this fee quacks a lot like an annual fee.

Cash Advance Fees

Watch out for this one! This fee represents the cost of cash advances from your credit card, and for some unknown reason, the interest rate is always considerably higher than what you pay as interest for purchases on your card. If you took a cash advance to buy something, it would be more costly to you than if you paid for the item directly through your card. Not only that, but the credit card company assesses an additional fee of anywhere between 2 percent and 4 percent of the amount you are obtaining as a cash advance as a Transaction Fee for Cash Advances just because they can. Add to this any surcharges applicable to getting the money from an ATM and you have a cost of borrowing money that would make Tony Soprano blush. And to make things worse, when you get a cash advance, there is never a grace period; so interest begins to accrue with the money still warm in your hand. And if that is not bad enough, most credit card companies will not even apply your monthly payment toward your high interest cash advance until the entire amount of any outstanding balances for purchases you have made using your credit card is paid off. If this makes cash advances on your credit card sound like a bad deal, there is a good reason for this. They are a bad deal.

Late Fees

Late fees are not just for libraries and video stores. Late fees represent a major source of income for credit card companies, with some late fees as high as $49. Late fees average around $15 for balances up to $100 and around $35 for account with balances of $1,000 or more. And with the average credit card debt at close to $9,000 per card-carrying household, most people who are late with their payments are paying that higher amount. According to the report "Borrowing to Make Ends Meet: The Growth of Credit Card Debt in the '90s," by Tamara Draut and Javier Silva of Demos, a non-partisan, non-profit public policy research and advocacy organization, late fees have rapidly become a large source of the profit for credit card issuers. According to their report, total industry revenue from late fees went from 1.7 billion dollars in 1996 to 7.3 billion dollars in 2001.

Over the Credit Line Fee

If you exceed your credit line, you will find yourself subject to a fee of around $29 even if your credit card company authorized the charge that put you over the top.

Transfer Fees

When you succumb to the never-ending offers to transfer your balance on one card to another card with a lower interest rate, you may not notice that the terms of your agreement often provide for a fee of as much as 3 percent of the amount of the debt you transfer.

Returned Payment Fee

If your check to the credit card company bounces, there is a fee of about $29 as a returned payment fee even if that same check is resubmitted and honored.

Fine Print Warning

You may find that you define the word "late" differently than the credit card company does. Unfortunately, they have the gold, so they make the rules (their version of the Golden Rule). This means that if your interpretations of that word collide, they win. Within the fine print of your credit card contract may be the specific time of day by which your monthly payment must be received in order to avoid a late fee. The Fair Credit Billing Act requires credit card companies to credit your account on the day that the payment is received. But the fine print, this time according to the law, permits the individual credit card company to make its own specific payment guidelines. If those guidelines are not met, the processing of your payment could be delayed by as much as five days, which can turn your timely payment into a late one.

Blocking

This is the name for the procedure by which a hold is put on a certain amount of your credit card's limit to cover anticipated expenses. For instance, when you check in to a hotel and the clerk runs your card through the machine, a block is put on your credit card for an amount equal to not just the cost of the room for the amount of time you will be staying at the hotel, but also for an amount representing the hotel's estimation of other anticipated costs of your stay, such as your food and bar bill. And remember to stay away from those tempting cashews in the mini-bar. They can cost you dearly. Another common place where blocking occurs is when you rent a car. Your credit card credit limit gets blocked for an amount of money that cover not just the cost of renting the car for the number of days you are expected to have the car, but also for anticipated gas bills as well. There is nothing illegal about blocking, but it is important to be aware of it because there are circumstances in which it can come back to haunt you. For instance, if you pay your bill with the same credit card you initially presented at check in, your actual charges will replace the blocked amount in a day or two. However, if you pay using a different credit card, the block may stay on and reduce your available credit on that card for as long as 15 days after you have settled with the hotel because the original credit card company is unaware that the final bill has been paid. Another problem is if you are close to your credit limit when you check in to the hotel, you may find yourself denied use of the credit card for other charges, such as meals outside the hotel or significant purchases, because your credit limit has been reached through the blocked amount.

Tip   *Use the same credit card both when you check in and when you check out of a hotel or when you initially reserve a rental car and when you pay for the car. And if you think that you may be close to your card's credit limit, merely ask the hotel or car leasing agency how much will be blocked.*

Payment Tip

Some credit card companies actually require you to use their own preprinted envelopes, but even if they do not, it is a good idea to do so in the interest of more efficient processing of your payment. Make sure you have included the billing coupon and have written clearly the amount that you are paying. Include your check, also written legibly, and remember to write your credit card account number on the check.

Payment Tip Two

When Ronald Reagan was running for President, he was asked what he was going to do to make the post office more efficient, to which he responded that he would start mailing postal workers their paychecks. Allow ample time when you send your check to the credit card company.

Tip   *Many people find that the greatest number of their bills, such as their mortgage or car payment, are due at the first of the month. If this places a burden on your ability to pay your credit card bill that may also be due at the first of the month, a simple way to avoid this problem is to just ask your credit card issuer to change the due date for your monthly payment. There is no harm in the asking, and many credit card issuers offer this ability to change the due date of your bill as an option. One important thing to remember, though, is that it may take a couple of billing cycles before this date change is fully implemented. It is important to make sure that your bill is paid promptly when due until your change of due date becomes effective. Otherwise, you could find yourself on the wrong side of a late fee.*

Other Terms with Which You Should Be Familiar

It was George Bernard Shaw who observed that "England and America are two countries divided by a common language." Unfortunately, when it comes to the language of credit cards, the language often is not commonly understood. These are a few of the terms with which you should be familiar.

Grace Period

This is an important item. It represents the period of time, most often between 20 and 25 days, during which you can pay your credit card bill without incurring interest charges. But it only applies if you pay your entire bill in full each and every month. By law, the credit card issuer must send you your monthly credit card statement of charges at least 14 days before the due date. If you carry any balance from month to month, interest will accrue. And (remember their Golden Rule) the grace period does not apply to cash advances.

Annual Percentage Rate (APR)

This is the interest rate as applied to the charges on your credit card. Your interest rate can be either a fixed rate or a variable rate although, realistically, they all are variable. A variable rate ties your interest rate each month to some standard, such as the U.S. Prime Rate as published in the *Wall Street Journal*. And don't think for a moment that your interest rate actually is at the Prime Rate. Rather, your credit card's interest rate is reached by adding a factor, such as 5.99 percent, to the Prime Rate to set your credit card interest rate. And if there is more than one U.S. Prime Rate published in the *Wall Street Journal*, guess which one is used to calculate your interest rate. You're right—the highest one.

Introductory Rate

This is a teaser rate. It is a temporary rate, often for as short a time as six months, which is used to lure you to a particular credit card. On the surface, it looks like a good deal—and it is, if you are a savvy credit card user. You can transfer your balance to a low interest card or a no interest card and take that time to catch up on your payments; however, if you default on any of the terms of your credit card agreement, you can suddenly find your credit card interest soaring from 0 percent to 28 percent. And what does it take to default? The obvious circumstance would be making a late payment or missing a payment altogether. However, buried within the fine print is the ability of the credit card company to declare you in default if you make a late payment to any other creditor you may have, be it another credit card, the telephone company, your mortgage, your car payment, or whatever.

Fixed Rate

A fixed rate is a bit of a misnomer because, although it does not carry the risk of automatically changing each month, it is only fixed for as long as the credit card company wants to leave it at a particular rate. The Federal Truth in Lending Act only requires that you be given 15 days notice before your fixed rate is changed, and there is no limit on the number of times they can change your rate. That sounds more like a broken rate to me than a fixed rate.

Calculating Your Monthly Finance Charges

How your interest rate is applied to your account in order to determine your finance charges can be calculated in one of three ways. The differences between the three can be significant to you. The manner in which your credit card company determines your finance charges may be found, again, buried in the fine print of your credit card agreement.

The first way is called "Adjusted Balance," and this is the most favorable to you. This way of calculating your finance charges takes your previous month's balance, adds any new charges you have made since the last statement, subtracts the amount of any payments you have made, and then multiplies this number by your monthly interest rate.

The second way of calculating your finance charges is called "Average Daily Balance." This is the most common of the three methods for calculating finance charges. It works by adding your charges and subtracting your payments daily as they occur and are reported. At the end of the billing period, the average of these daily computations is determined and your interest rate is applied to this figure.

The final way of calculating your finance charges, and one that is most favorable to the credit card company, is the "Previous Balance" method by which the credit card company takes your previous month's statement and multiplies it by your interest rate to arrive at your new finance charge. This is more advantageous to the credit card company because using this method permits the credit card company to charge you interest on balances that you have already reduced.

Because the individual banks participating in their respective programs issue their own MasterCard and Visa credit cards, the interest rates and terms may differ significantly from card to card within the same card program. The terms offered to various people by the same bank may even differ due to the credit-worthiness and desirability of particular customers.

Tip   *It is probably good advice anyway, but in order to avoid a default that would cause your credit card interest rate to rise to the stratosphere, it is a good practice to pay all your bills promptly when you receive them. You may even wish to pay your bills electronically for extra speed. If you disagree with a particular bill you receive, act promptly to resolve the dispute to keep it from becoming a cause for declaring you in default on your credit card contract. It is much easier to prevent this problem from occurring than having to fight your credit card company to convince them that you are not at fault for a late payment.*

Pre-approved

Wow! Without even asking for it, you have received a notice from another credit card company saying that based upon your stellar credit record you have been pre-approved for a higher credit limit than you presently have. A pre-approved credit card offer starts when the credit card company obtains lists from the major credit reporting agencies of people who meet certain criteria, such as total outstanding debt and the number of open credit accounts. The people on these lists are then solicited for new credit cards. It is not until you actually respond in the affirmative, which is lawyer-talk for saying "yes" to their offer, that the credit card company actually first looks at your credit report. If your eyes are strong enough to read the fine print of your credit card offer, you will note that although you have been pre-approved for the new card, you are not actually pre-approved for that fantastic interest rate or other terms loudly proclaimed in the initial solicitation you received. Rather, the credit card company reserves the right to examine your credit report and completed application to determine the actual terms they will offer you, which may turn out to be a somewhat less favorable interest rate or a significantly lower credit limit. In fact, they can decide to reject your application altogether. So much for pre-approved. In addition, within the fine print you may be surprised to see that the interest rate for which you actually qualify may be even higher than what you are presently paying. If you agree to transfer your entire present credit card debt to this new card, you will be paying even more interest than you were before. Not a very good deal.

Warning   *Rip, shred, and tear apart any pre-approval letters that you decide not to act upon, because they are fodder for identity thieves to easily establish credit in your name.*

Tip   *If you don't want to receive pre-approved credit card offers, all you need to do is make a single telephone call to the Opt Out Request Line, 1-888-567-8688, and request that your name be removed from the mailing lists of the three major credit reporting bureaus: Equifax, Experian, and Trans Union. This one call will lessen your junk mail, reduce your chances of becoming a victim of identity theft, and perhaps even save a tree.*

Secured Cards

People who may otherwise not be able to qualify for a standard credit card may find that they are eligible for a secured credit card, which requires that the credit card holder have a bank deposit with the card-issuing bank. This deposit is used to guarantee or secure the payment of the credit card bills. The line of credit of the credit card is closely related to that bank account, which can be reached by the bank if the credit card holder fails to pay his or her monthly credit card bill. The responsible use of a secured MasterCard or Visa may enable someone to establish a good enough credit record to enable him or her to become eligible for a standard, unsecured credit card. Secured credit cards do not differ in appearance from unsecured credit cards in any way, so there is no stigma to using one.

Debit Card

A debit card is not really a credit card although it very much looks like one, right down to the Visa or MasterCard logo. However, it allows you to access your checking account through the simple use of the debit card without having to carry checks. Also, because a debit card facilitates immediate access to your checking account, it is important to remember that you do not get the 20 to 25 day grace period you have with a credit card between the time that the debt was incurred and the time that it becomes due. Although a debit card is quite convenient, it does not come with the same legal protection inherent in a credit card transaction, such as the limitation on unauthorized use. However, the Electronic Funds Transfer Act limits your liability to $50 of unauthorized charges if notification to the card-issuing bank is given within two business days of discovering that your card is missing. Failure to notify the bank within two days of becoming aware of the theft or loss of your card can raise your potential liability to $500. If you fail to notify your bank within 60 days of receiving a monthly statement that indicates unauthorized withdrawals, you can be held responsible for all of the fraudulent charges. With a standard credit card, you are only generally responsible for no more than $50 of unauthorized charges, and if you report the card as lost or stolen before the card is used by anyone else, you will not be liable for any unauthorized charges.

Tip   *If your card is missing or stolen, report the loss of the card immediately by telephone to the credit card issuer and follow up the notification with a letter sent certified mail, return receipt requested.*

Personal Identification Number (PIN)

This is the password you choose to enable you to use your credit card or debit card at Automatic Teller Machines (ATMs). Usually a PIN consists of four numbers, although George Costanza's in *Seinfeld* was five numbers, the letters of which on a keypad spelled out the word "Bosco." In case your card is lost or stolen, it is a good idea not to write down your PIN or to pick an obvious number, such as the numerical designation of your birthday.

Extra Card Benefits

The credit card business is a competitive business with many institutions seeking your business. Different credit cards offer a dazzling array of additional benefits to ownership of their particular cards. Your own personal preferences will help determine which card is right for you. Some of the bells and whistles are detailed in the following paragraphs.

Cash Back

With cash back, the card issuer refunds a portion of the cost of your credit card purchases to you. But as you might expect, this particular benefit is fraught with conditions and limitations. Some cards pay you a certain amount on every dollar you charge, while others rebate at a higher rate when you charge more. Most credit cards limit how much you can be refunded annually, and, within the fine print, the card issuers reserve the right to change the rules of the cash-back program whenever they choose.

Extended Warranty

The card issuer extends the warranty of products purchased with the card. This can be particularly helpful.

Purchase Protection

Stolen or accidentally damaged products purchased with the card are replaced within a certain period of time.

Travel Discounts

Hotel and car rental discounts may be available in some circumstances.

Rental Car Insurance

This benefit can be particularly attractive. It covers the cost of auto rental loss and damage when you rent a car. Check with your credit card company before you travel to make sure you are not stumped when the clerk at the automobile leasing company asks you whether you want the optional coverage and attempts to scare you into paying for its own overpriced coverage.

Online Fraud Protection

Some credit cards promise to not hold you responsible for any unauthorized charges made through online purchases.

Reward Plans

Under these programs, your purchases provide you with points that can be redeemed for merchandise, services, or can even be transferred to frequent traveler programs of hotels or frequent flier programs of the various airlines. Reward plans differ from greatly from card to card. Some even provide preferential tickets to theater or sporting events. I got early tickets to the original run of *The Producers* on Broadway through a program of my American Express card. The rewards offered through the various reward programs can be quite elaborate. The American Express Platinum Card Membership Rewards Program had a Wimbledon package for a mere 1,160,000 points that offered tickets to the 2004 Wimbledon Tennis Tournament. The package included personal commentary on the action by former Wimbledon Champion Stan Smith, tours of the grounds, meals, accommodations, and even tennis lessons from Smith and other professional tennis players.

Some credit card companies even permit you to use your reward points toward reducing your mortgage. The Citibank Home Rebate Platinum Select MasterCard allows you to tie your rewards points toward your mortgage loan.

The sky is the limit with some rewards programs. Or is it? American Express actually allows cardholders to redeem their points for zero-gravity flight, edge of space flight, or even sub-orbital space flight. These offers are available through American Express's relationship with Space Adventures Ltd., a company that calls itself "the world's leading space flight experiences and space tourism company." With ties to the Russian space program, Space Adventures Ltd. provides an opportunity for card holders to exchange their reward points for a sub-orbital space flight at an altitude of at least 62 miles, similar to the early flights of Astronauts Alan Shepard and Gus Grissom, for a mere 20 million points. For more budget-conscious cardholders, edge of space flight in a MIG jet at speeds of Mach 2.5 at an altitude of 80,000 feet are available for a mere three million reward points. And zero-gravity flight in specially outfitted jets that are used to train cosmonauts can be had for the bargain cost of a million reward points.

The theory behind the rewards programs is simple. The credit card issuer wants to encourage you to use the card as much as possible so that they will receive more fees from participating merchants while the benefit to card holders is obvious—you get something for nothing. Or do you? As with all such programs, if you are spending money to buy things you do not really need just to run up your points, it may not be such a great deal. Nor is it a particularly good deal if you end up paying high interest carrying costs if you do not pay off your balance each month. Do the math.

A good place to go to compare an array of different credit cards is bankrate.com. This is an excellent website for all kinds of financial information that is quite consumer friendly. It also has a place where you can get all the information you need to compare different credit cards to determine which is the best for you.

Picking a Card

When the first automobiles were manufactured at the beginning of the twentieth century choosing a color was easy. Black was your only option. Now you have a myriad of choices. I don't even know what taupe is, but I know it is a color option for my car. Your credit card may not come in taupe, but then again maybe it does because there are thousands of choices of credit cards and there are many more variables than just the color of the card. So how do you choose a credit card? Some of the basic considerations are as follows:

1. Will you be paying off your balance every month or carrying a balance? If you are paying off your entire balance every month, the interest rate is irrelevant. If, on the other hand, you are pretty sure that you will not be paying off your entire balance each month, the interest rate is probably the most important factor in choosing a card. Also, make sure you understand the charges for cash advances.

2. Is your interest rate fixed or variable, and if it is variable, to what index is it tied?

3. If you are considering a card with a teaser rate, are you familiar with the conditions that can cause you to lose that teaser rate and what your interest rate will be if and when it does get bumped up?

4. Does your card have and annual fee? Generally, the lower the interest rate, the more likely the card is to have an annual fee.

5. How is the minimum payment calculated? (However, you should almost always try to pay more than the minimum payment for reasons I will discuss later.)

6. If you are transferring balances from other credit cards to your new card, what are the fees and conditions for doing so?

7. In addition to the annual fee, what other fees and penalties are connected with the card's use?

Gold Cards

There's gold in them there cards. Many people during the California gold rush of 1849 lost their money falling for the come-on that there was "gold in them thar hills." Striking gold, many of them found out, was not as easy as they thought. Today, people still fall prey to the allure of gold when it comes to their credit cards, and it appears that many of them end up with fool's gold. You may find yourself inundated with offers for gold credit cards that imply that they are prestigious as well as providing special services or features. All too often, these representations are false. Until the late 1990s, gold cards were somewhat selective and did provide a certain level of prestige, for whatever that was worth. Since that time, however, the platinum card has taken over and the gold card does not generally represent either elite status or significant benefits. In fact, according to bankrate.com, the average interest rates for fixed rate gold cards are higher than the average interest rate for standard fixed rate credit cards. Learn to be colorblind. Ignore the color of the card you are considering and carefully evaluate its terms, conditions, and features.

Zero Interest Credit Cards

It does not seem like it could get any better than that—a credit card that does not charge you interest to borrow money—but of course there is a catch. When my children were little they invented the word "Yeahbut." This word was often used by them at the start of their response after being asked if they had done something that they were not supposed to have done. Said quickly, the two words "yeah" and "but" became one word that generally preceded an explanation as to why things were not as they seemed. I have adopted this word, and you should too, when it comes to zero interest credit cards. Are zero interest credit cards great? "Yeah but" there are some significant flaws to these cards.

Zero interest credit cards are used by credit card issuers to lure you to their card by offering to have your present outstanding balance, which for most households is around $8,400, transferred to their card to be paid off at zero percent interest, sometimes for a specific period, such as six months, but sometimes for as long as the life of the loan. Common conditions for these zero interest cards include being required to use the card for purchases every month at certain minimum dollar amounts. Remember, the purchases you charge anew on your card may not be for that teaser rate of zero percent at any time. Of course, if you fail to meet any of the terms or conditions of the zero percent agreement, suddenly you may find your interest rate on the transferred balance reaching up to a level greater than the drinking age. Merely being late with your payment to the credit card company or, as I explained earlier, being late on any of your bills regardless of to whom you owe them, may result in the zero interest rate being lost forever.

Ideally, your zero percent interest rate would stay with you for the entire time it took you to pay off of your transferred balance from your previous credit card, but any payments that you make on the card are first applied to reduce the transferred balance. The amounts you charge presently on your new card are subject to whatever the interest rate is for new purchases. And this figure might be significantly higher than the zero percent you are carrying for your transferred balance. So, as your balance on the card for new purchases increases, carrying with it a higher interest rate, you may still find yourself with a great deal of high interest rate debt after having paid off the transferred balance.

So, for whom is the zero interest rate card good? If you are able to meet the minimum present monthly card usage requirements without running up additional charges on the card and you pay off your transferred balance relatively quickly without ever being late on a payment to the card issuer or anyone else, the offer may be worth grabbing.

Credit Where Credit Is Due

One reason many people use credit cards is that it is easier to dispute a purchase if you receive defective goods or services. When you return goods that fail to live up to their warranty, a credit will be issued to your credit card account. If you have been paying off your balance in full each month, you will have a positive credit balance on your card. Federal law provides you with the right to choose to either have the credit stay as a credit on your credit card to be applied to future purchases or past balances or to have the money refunded to you by the credit card company. To obtain a refund from your credit card company, all you have to do is ask for it and they must send you a check within seven business days.

9

FINE PRINT

Reading fine print is important. Of course, there is nothing "fine" about fine print. It should be called what it really is, which is "very small print of confusing language." The print contained in credit card agreements is so small that recently I was trying to read a credit card agreement and the print was so small that I went searching for my reading glasses until I realized I was already wearing them. In any event, as much of a task as this represents, everyone would be well served by reading their credit card agreements. Perhaps to make this task seem less tedious you should think of this as a word game—a game that you win when you spot the tricks and legal scams contained therein.

What Interest Rate Will You Pay?

With laws limiting interest rates (usury laws) why are some credit card interest rates so high? The answer is that only about half of the states have usury laws. The other states place no limit on credit card interest rates. Guess in which states most credit card issuers are located? You win. Or maybe you lose. If a company based in a state without interest rate limits issued your credit card, you may have to pay an interest rate on your card that exceeds the rate allowed by your state's law. As I indicated in Chapter 8, for this you have the United States Supreme Court to thank. In a 1978 case, Marquette National Bank of Minneapolis vs. First Omaha Service Corp., the court ruled that banks could charge whatever rates are allowed in their home states to customers who may live in other states that limit interest rates. For this reason, so many credit card issuers are based in North Dakota, Delaware, and Nebraska—states with laws favorable to lenders.

Diogenes Would Be Proud

The ancient Greek philosopher Diogenes was said to have spent his time trying to find an honest man. If Diogenes had read the fine print on one particular credit card agreement, he would have had to admit, he had found that person, even if that honesty was not coupled with charity toward one's fellow man. The particular section of the agreement says: "Payment Allocation: We will allocate your payments and credits in a way that is most favorable to us." Well, at least they are not lying to us.

While you are looking at that fine print, check out the minimum monthly payment requirement. For a long time, credit card companies required cardholders to pay at least five percent of their outstanding balances each month. However, in recent years, many of those credit card companies have quietly lowered that amount to two percent. While at first blush that might seem to be in the consumer's favor, in reality it was done to prolong the credit card holder's debt and increase the overall interest the credit card company receives over time. For example, a person carrying an $8,000 balance at an 18% interest rate will take over 50 years to pay off the debt with 2% minimum monthly payments.

Late Fees

In the classic television detective series *Columbo*, which starred Peter Falk, Lieutenant Columbo always seemed to be distracted and disorganized, but in reality he was extremely focused and observant. One common scene that brought delight to fans of the show was when Columbo left a room in which he had been speaking to the murderer. He kept turning around and starting question after question with, "Oh, just one more thing..." Then he trapped the criminal. Well, the credit card companies are not Lieutenant Columbo and we consumers are certainly not murderers, but when it comes to trapping us in the fine print of their credit card agreements, it always seems like there is "just one more thing." Your monthly payment is due on whatever date of the month it says on your credit card bill. If your payment is late, the fine print of your credit card agreement provides for the right of the credit card company to assess a late fee, which can be as much as $35 for each late payment. In the past, some credit card companies gave their customers five or even ten days of grace after the due date before assessing a penalty, but that is not the situation any longer. So you send your payment with sufficient time to arrive at the credit card company on your bill's due date. But, just one more thing: Some credit card companies deem your payment late if it is processed later than 1:00 p.m. on the day of your due date. Some credit card companies don't receive and process mail until after 1:00 p.m.; therefore, the real date by which your monthly payment must be received is a day earlier than the date indicated on your contract. So you need to make sure your payment gets there three days ahead of the due date. But just one more thing: If the envelope contains a staple, a paper clip, or a note from you, the fine print of the contract specifies that there may be a delay of up to five days in posting your payment. This might cause a late payment to be assessed on a payment that arrived at the credit card company prior to the due date of the bill. I'll bet Lieutenant Columbo read the fine print before sending in his payment.

Another problem with late payments is that they can also trigger penalty interest rates as high as 29%; so, for example, instead of the 10% interest rate your card may carry, your rate will now be jacked up to 29% effective immediately. In fact, even if you are timely in your credit card payment, credit card companies generally reserve the right to raise your rate to a penalty rate if you are late with any other payment to any of your creditors, whoever they may be. Just read the fine print.

Avoiding Late Fees

Murphy's Law says that what can go wrong, will go wrong, and that axiom certainly applies to the situation that occurs when you send your monthly credit card payment by mail to the card issuer. Mail can be lost. Mail can be delayed. And after your payment arrives at the credit card company, the opportunity for being misplaced, despite the proverb, can knock more than once. An easy solution to this problem is to pay your credit card bill online. Many credit card issuers, such as Citibank, MBNA, and American Express, permit you to enroll in online payment plans directly with them, while all the others welcome online payments through the many online payment services, such as you can find on Quicken.

Tip   *If the due date for your monthly credit card payment does not match up well with your cash flow for the month, many credit card companies will simply let you change the due date for your credit card payment to a date you prefer.*

It's the Fees

More and more, it is the fees that are a major source of revenue for the credit card companies. Late fees, cash advance fees, over the limit fees, and the remaining myriad fine print fees are becoming a sneaky little profit center. Between the years of 1995 and 1999, the total fee income of credit card companies went up 158% to 21.4 billion dollars. And during the year 2000, income derived from fees accounted for a quarter of the total credit card income for the credit card companies.[1]

Late fees have increased by 112% between 1992 and 2000 according to a 1999 Credit Card Survey by Consumer Action (www.consumer-action.org).

Cash Advances

As I described in detail in Chapter 8, the interest rate and fees for cash advances are particularly outrageous and buried within the fine print. It is not unusual for the interest rate for cash advances to be as much as twice the interest rate for purchases made using your credit card. In addition, grace periods generally do not apply to cash advances, so you are responsible for interest as soon as you take the cash advance even if you pay the entire credit card bill on the day you receive your monthly bill. Adding insult to injury, there also may be a transaction fee in addition to the interest.

Credit Card Disability Coverage

Disability insurance may be one of the least used and most important types of insurance coverage available today. However, not all disability insurance is created equal. Read the fine print. Some programs defer your monthly payments, but they fail to forgive any amounts owed. The outstanding balance on your credit card will continue to accrue compound interest during a time when you cannot even use your card.

Advance Fee Cards

Legitimate credit card companies do not charge you for a credit card under any circumstances until you are approved for the particular card. Illegitimate credit card sellers will promise people with less than stellar credit access to credit cards with great terms "for a fee." It's a scam.

What Happens When Your Credit Card Is Sold?

Admit it. All too often when we get a piece of mail from our credit card issuer, when we see that it is not a bill, we consider it junk mail and throw it out without even reading it. But that is not a good thing to do. That letter may contain a notification that your credit card account has been sold to another bank. In that case, the bank's version of the Golden Rule applies; they have the gold, or in some cases the platinum, so they make the rules. One of the first things you may notice is that suddenly the relatively low interest rate you may have had has jumped up to a rate so high that the law in your home state would prohibit it. But remember, because the law of the state where the credit card company is located controls the interest rate that may be charged, you may find the less-savory consumer laws of Arkansas, North Dakota, or Delaware controlling the rate.

Late fees may also be increased when your card is sold. You may find that there is no grace period for late payments. You also may find, buried in the fine print, that if you are one of those smart people who pay off your credit card in full each month, the interest-free period of 25 days to which you have become accustomed has been changed to as little as 15 days. Some particularly unlucky people may find that the interest on new purchases kicks in at the moment of purchase, so there is never an interest-free period.

There is little you can do if your credit card account is sold other than to try to negotiate better terms, which is a hard sell. Your alternative is to close the account and find yourself a new card with better terms and hope that it does not get sold to another bank. If you do close your account, you can continue to pay off your balance at the old rate of your former card. In that case, remember to make arrangements for automatic monthly charges such as a gym membership or Internet bill that might be charged to your credit card to be paid from another source. Otherwise, any further charges made on your credit card will trigger the new higher credit card rate for your entire account.

Oh, You Tease

According to the Public Interest Research Group, short-term, low-interest teaser rates are common ways that credit card companies market their cards. The PIRG study found that of 100 credit card offers studied, fifty-seven advertised extremely low interest rates that rose 264% within seven months. Although the short-term, low-interest rate was prominently featured in the credit card companies' solicitations, the future raising of that rate was buried within the fine print.

ᴥ Roberts vs. Fleet Bank

In 1999 Denise Roberts received a credit card solicitation in the mail from Fleet Bank similar to some that many of you have undoubtedly received as well. The letter, offering a "Titanium MasterCard" (sounds even mightier than Kryptonite), promised a 7.99 percent fixed APR for both purchases and balance transfers. Twice within the letter it emphasized that the rate "was NOT an introductory rate" and said that the rate "won't go up in just a few short months." Just as an aside, other than February, how many short months are there? In any event, Ms. Roberts filled out the "Pre-Qualified Invitation" and received the card in June of 1999 with a 7.99 percent interest rate, as promised. However, in July of 2000 Fleet raised the "fixed" rate to 10.5 percent. Denise Roberts sued under the Federal Truth in Lending Act arguing that Fleet had not clearly and conspicuously disclosed its right to change the APR whenever it wished. Fleet responded by saying that in its cardholder agreement sent to Denise Roberts with the actual credit card in June of 1999 was language (albeit in very fine print unlike the bold lettering of their original customer solicitation)— that said specifically, "My agreement terms (including rates) are subject to change." Oh, yeah, that is a real clear disclosure. Fortunately, the Third Circuit Court of Appeals disagreed with Fleet and said that the bank's disclosures "read in conjunction with the solicitation materials present a material issue of fact as whether the bank clearly and conspicuously disclosed its right to change the APR." Regardless of how this case is ultimately decided (the decision of the Third Circuit only involved initial motions of Fleet to end the case in its favor without even having a trial), the most important lesson to take from this case is the importance of carefully reading the cardholder agreement, no matter how indecipherable it may appear.

Risk-Based Pricing

When you receive a "pre-approved" offer from a credit card company, you are not actually approved for the low interest rate prominently featured within the written offer. In fact, you may not even be approved for the card on any terms. It is entirely dependent upon your completed application and a review of your all-important credit report. But even if you are eventually approved for a credit card to be issued by the particular credit card company soliciting your business, you are in no way guaranteed the alluring interest rate first waved in your face by their original letter to you. The interest rate on the card that you are ultimately offered, as well as other terms of the contract, can differ significantly, and not necessarily in your favor, from the terms you were led to believe were a done deal.

After you have completed your application, the credit card company reviews the information you provided, your credit report, and your overall FICO score to decide the terms of the credit card that will be offered to you. The range of interest rates charged by the particular credit card issuer can often vary by as much as 12%. The rate on the card that is sent to you along with the written terms of the credit card will be based on the credit card issuer's assessment of the risk you present as a customer. The lower they perceive their risk to be, the more favorable the terms you will be offered. Unfortunately, you have no input in this process after sending in your application. Opening the envelope with your new credit card is like opening your stocking on Christmas morning. You may find a lump of coal in it in the form of a much higher interest rate than you anticipated, or you may find the present for which you had been hoping. If the surprise when you open that envelope is an interest rate or other terms that are unacceptable to you, you are not bound to accept that credit card. You can choose to just not activate it, or you can call the credit card company to attempt to negotiate more favorable terms.

Tip *With risk-based pricing, the interest rate on the card that you are actually offered is dependent on information contained in your credit report, so you should consider getting a copy of your credit report to make sure it is accurate before applying for a credit card. (This also applies to a mortgage or car loan or any other loan dependent upon your FICO score.)*

Transferring Balances

Everyone is tempted at one time or another to transfer his or her balance on a high interest credit card to another card with a significantly lower interest rate. Sometimes you do not even have to open the envelope from the credit card company to know what a great deal they are offering. Right there on the outside of the envelope, enticing you to open it is a proclamation that you can get this new credit card at interest rates so low it makes your wallet spin. Sometimes they even offer you a zero percent interest for a period of time. Those credit card companies sure must love us to make us such tremendous offers. However, the fine print is not quite as appealing. First of all, the so-called teaser rate may last only a few months, and if you make a mistake and are late with a payment, all bets are off and they jack up your interest rate to a figure greater than the voting age. And even though the letter says you are pre-approved for this great teaser rate of zero percent, again the fine print says that the actual rate that they will offer you depends on their analysis of your completed application. As Gomer Pyle used to say, "Surprise, surprise." Many people who receive those envelopes with the teaser rates on the outside do not qualify for that rate. Instead, they are given a higher interest rate.

What does it cost you to transfer your balance from the old credit card to the new card? Again, you have to read the fine print to learn whether they have balance transfers fees, which are often between three and five percent of the amount you are transferring. Sometimes they have a cap and sometimes they do not.

The Ultimate Trap

Perhaps the ultimate trap occurs when you transfer an outstanding balance from your old credit card to your new credit card without realizing that the transfer can take as long as a month to be completed. When you get your monthly statement from the credit card whose balance you are transferring, you may make the mistake of choosing to ignore it because you know that it is being paid off through your new credit card. But if the transfer has not yet been completed, you face possible late fees from your old card and the possibility of your new card raising your interest rate for not being current with all your credit obligations.

Is It Always a Good Deal Even If I Get the Advertised Rate?

Assuming that you actually get the low interest rate that is indicated in the pre-approval letter sent to you, there may be other conditions. For instance, the new low interest rate may only apply to the balance that you transfer from your previous credit card. You also may be required to make a certain number of purchases monthly on your new card; and when you make your regular monthly payment, it may be totally applied to the transferred low interest balance so that your new charges just grow and grow.

More Fine Print in the Balance Transfer Agreement

What if you get a low interest rate on your transfers for a teaser period of six months, but you fully understand that and take that time to make substantial payments toward your transferred balance at the low teaser rate? Isn't that a good deal? Not necessarily. Buried within the fine print of some balance transfer contracts are provisions that require you to pay off the entire balance transferred within the teaser period. Otherwise, you are charged at your new credit card's regular rate (which is generally significantly higher than your teaser rate) for the entire teaser period. So if you transferred $10,000 and paid off all but $50 of it over the six-month teaser rate period, some plans would retroactively assess the regular purchase interest rate of your new card for the entire teaser period on the full $10,000 transferred.

Golden Rule—Credit Card Style

Remember the credit card companies' version of the Golden Rule, that they have the gold so they make the rules? When you transfer a balance from one credit card to another, if you default on the terms of the new card's credit card agreement, you can be subject to a huge increase in your interest rate. You may be relatively unconcerned because you fully intend to make your payments regularly and on time. But what if you miss a payment? It happens. The bill might be misplaced, or perhaps you were sick when the monthly bill was due. In that case, you might find yourself paying a huge interest rate on your transferred balance as well as new charges. And remember that many credit card agreements have fine print that provides that you are in default and subject to an increase in your interest rate if you merely owe miss a payment to any of your creditors. Are you willing to take that risk?

The Only Thing Certain Is Change

It is a truism that the only thing that remains constant is change, and that certainly applies to your credit card agreement. If you read the fine print, you will notice that they can change the terms of your agreement any damn time they please. That means that your interest rate, as well as the charges and fees connected with your card, may be changed whenever the credit card issuer chooses to do so.

When the credit card company notifies you about changes to the terms of your credit card agreement, it will likely look like junk mail that you receive regularly from other credit card companies and ignore.

What should you do? As much as it is a pain in the neck, it is important to carefully read everything that you get from your credit card issuer. The consequences of your failure to do so can be harmful to your fiscal health. Many people who fail to read the change of terms notices never even observe that the interest rate on their card has gone up. This failure costs you money.

A Light at the End of the Tunnel

Sometimes that light at the end of the tunnel is an oncoming train, but sometimes that light is your bright financial future. Buried within the fine print of your credit card agreement in the section that pertains to changing the terms of the agreement is a provision that actually says that you have the right to not accept the changes the credit card company is making. You are generally required to notify the credit card company in writing of your refusal to accept the new terms of your credit card within a specific period of time, which is a good reason to carefully read any written communications you receive from your credit card company. Usually, if you refuse to accept the new terms, you must stop using that credit card. However, you also usually have the ability to continue to pay off the outstanding balance under the terms and conditions to which you have previously agreed. This means that if the interest rate or other fees are being changed (and don't expect those changes ever to be to your benefit) you can continue to pay off your debt under the former interest rate, which can significantly work to your benefit.

A Few Things to Remember

If you determine that you do not want to stay with your credit card company under the new terms they are requiring, it is imperative that you not use your credit card after receiving notice of the proposed changes. As when your credit card account is sold to another bank, use of the card constitutes agreement to the new terms according to the fine print in your credit card agreement. In addition, make sure that you notify the credit card company promptly and in the method specifically prescribed within your credit card agreement of your refusal to accept the change of terms.

A Tip

It never hurts to ask. If you have been a good customer and you receive a notice of change of terms, call the credit card company and see if you can negotiate better terms. There is a lot of competition for credit card customers, and they do not want to lose you if you have been a good customer. Tell them that you are inclined to close the account and not accept the changes they are proposing. See if they are willing to negotiate some better terms with you related to the interest rate, fees, or whatever would be meaningful to you. You have nothing to lose.

Their Holiday Gift to You

What good buddies the credit card companies are to us. It is not uncommon to receive a notice from them around Christmas time that we can skip a payment. On the surface that sounds like a generous offer by the credit card company; in reality, the interest owed on your purchases continues to compound. If you take them up on their "generous" offer, you will end up just increasing your balance owed.

Gambling with Your Credit Cards

Many people consider credit cards a form of gambling, so perhaps it is poetic justice that within the fine print of some credit card agreements are specific provisions that charge you a three percent fee on the total amount of your purchase of lottery tickets or casino gaming chips. Using your credit card at the casino can be a much more expensive proposition than you might think at the time.

Fair Credit Billing Act

The Fair Credit Billing Act (FCBA) applies if you are billed for items you never received, such as when you are the victim of identity theft and someone has accessed your credit card. It also applies when you are

- Billed for goods that you ordered, but never received

- Charged more than the agreed upon price

- Charged for products that are defective or do not work as represented

---

⁌ Loophole

The law generally limits your responsibility for charges on your credit card to no more than $50 for charges that you did not authorize.

In order to avail yourself of the protections provided by the FCBA, you must first try to resolve the matter with the merchant from whom the product was bought. In addition, according to the letter of the law, the cost of the product must be over $50 and the sale must have taken place either in the state in which you live or within 100 miles of your home. In reality, these restrictions are rarely, if ever, enforced.

When you find yourself unable to resolve your differences with the merchant you paid by credit card, you may then contact your credit card company to request that it withhold payment. The credit card company then typically issues a temporary credit to your account so that you are not charged for the goods or services. In addition, the credit card company is required by law to suspend any finance charges on that particular disputed purchase. The credit card company then contacts the merchant directly and investigates the matter. Within 30 days of receiving your written complaint, your credit card company must contact you, in writing, acknowledging receipt of your complaint. By law, they have two billing cycles, but no more than 90 days, within which to complete their investigation. After the investigation is completed, if the credit card company agrees with you, the temporary credit becomes permanent; however, if they determine that the merchant was correct, you will be billed the full amount of the purchase on your credit card along with the usual finance charges.

Tip *Leave a paper trail. Go back to the merchant as soon as you discover a problem. If he is not willing to satisfy you, send your complaint to the company in writing by certified mail, return receipt requested. Make sure that you include not only the details of the purchase and your complaint, but also the details of your discussion with the store employees when you attempted to return the merchandise. Make sure to include the date you went back to the store, the name of the person with whom you spoke, and the substance of your discussion. When you make your request of the credit card company to withhold payment of the charge for that item, include with your request a copy of your letter to the merchant as well as copies of any documentation to support your claim, such as receipts or sales slips. Do not send original documents to the credit card company. Again, make sure you send your letter to your credit card company by certified mail, return receipt requested.*

Check the Address

Make sure that you send your letter to the credit card company at the proper address. Your credit card agreement contains the specific appropriate address for billing inquiries. This is not the same address to which you send your payments.

Critical Information

Just like when telling a good joke, timing is everything. In order to make a proper demand for non-payment of a disputed charge on your credit card, your communication to your credit card company must be done in writing within 60 days of when the bill with the disputed charge was sent to you. Remember, that is 60 days from when the credit card company sends the bill to you, not 60 days from when you actually receive the bill. However, you are not required to report unauthorized charges that arise, such as when you are the victim of identity within a particular time frame.

Picky Little Detail

Although during the investigation period by the credit card company you are not required to pay for the disputed item, the credit card company may apply the amount of the disputed purchase against your credit limit, thereby reducing your available credit.

Affect on Your Credit Rating

While your claim is being investigated, the merchant may not report the matter as a delinquent bill to the credit reporting agencies. They may, however, report the matter as a bill being challenged. This notation will not affect your credit score or any application for credit you may have pending during this period.

What If the Investigation Rules Against You?

If the credit card company rules that you owe the bill, they must provide you with a written explanation as to their reasoning. They must also provide you with copies of any relevant documents, if you request them. You are now responsible for payment of the disputed charge as well as any finance charges on the purchase that had been suspended.

Fine Print in Your Favor

If the credit card company neglects to meet the time requirements of the Fair Credit Billing Act, either by acknowledging your complaint more than 30 days after you have notified them of the dispute or taking too long to complete their investigation, you may not be held responsible for the first $50 of the disputed bill. This is true even if it is determined that the charges were legitimate.

Endnotes

1. "Fee Income." July 2000. www.cardweb.com/trak/pastissues/july00.html.

10

PROTECTION FROM CREDIT DISCRIMINATION

C ontrary to what we would like to believe, love does not make the world go round. And since 2003, neither does money. Credit makes the world go round. Americans now use debit cards and credit cards more than cash and checks to pay for everything from groceries to gas to the speeding ticket you get on the way home from the store with your groceries. Anyone without access to credit is at a distinct disadvantage in today's world, so protecting people from discrimination in regard to credit is of great importance.

The Equal Credit Opportunity Act

Congress enacted the Equal Credit Opportunity Act in 1974 with the intention of protecting and extending the credit rights of women. At that time, many unmarried women had difficulty getting credit without having a co-signer, and many married women found that they needed their husbands to join in on any credit applications. Coverage under the law was later expanded. It now protects people from discrimination in regard to sex, age, marital status, race, color, national origin, or whether you receive public assistance throughout the credit process.

Specifically, the law prohibits creditors from inquiring about

1. Your sex, race, color, religion, or national origin

2. Your plans for having children

3. Your marital status, unless you live in a community property state

4. Whether or not you receive alimony or child support, unless you intend to include that income as income available to you to repay credit extended to you

The law further prohibits creditors from

1. Refusing to consider pension income, Social Security payments, and wages from part-time work or annuity payments in determining your eligibility for credit

2. Assuming that a woman will stop working outside the home in order to raise a child and thereby have her income reduced

Creditors are allowed to ask about the following:

1. How many people you are responsible for supporting

2. Whether you pay alimony or child support, although they are not allowed to ask whether you receive alimony or child support unless you want to have that income counted in determining your eligibility for credit

Voluntary Disclosures for Monitoring Purposes

If you are applying for a mortgage, the lender will ask you about your ethnicity, race, and sex. Answering is totally voluntary and is used by the federal government to monitor the lender's compliance with equal credit opportunity, fair housing, and home mortgage disclosure laws. The categories for ethnicity are

1. Hispanic or Latino

2. Not Hispanic or Latino

The categories for race are

1. American Indian or Alaska Native

2. Native Hawaiian or other Pacific Islander

3. Asian

4. White

5. Black or African American

What the Law Does and Does Not Do

Although the law protects people within the classes protected by the Equal Credit Opportunity Act from being discriminated against in regard to credit, it does not guarantee that you will automatically qualify for a credit card, mortgage, or other application for credit. As always, your income, debts, and credit score are all important in the determination of whether or not you will be granted credit.

The law does, however, require that if you are turned down for credit or granted credit at less favorable terms than generally offered, you receive an explanation of why your credit application was treated as it was. After you have filed a completed credit application, the law says that the creditor has as long as 30 days to act on your application and inform you as to whether your application for credit was accepted or rejected. If your application for credit is rejected, you have a right to be told the reasons for that determination. Some creditors will tell you the reasons within the rejection letter, while others will provide you with a toll-free telephone number or an address to contact to inquire as to the reasons for your application's rejection.

Tip *If you do receive a rejection letter following a credit application, it is important not to delay in asking for the reasons for the rejection because the law only gives you 60 days to request this information.*

The reasons given by the creditor must be specific, such as your income was too low to qualify or your credit report shows continuous late payments. When you have this information, you will be in a better position to evaluate whether the reason you were rejected for the loan is legitimate. Much inaccurate information appears on credit reports, and your application for credit may have been turned down due to false information that might appear on your credit report. At this point, under the Fair and Accurate Credit Transactions Act (FACT), you will be in a position to correct inaccurate or misleading information that may appear on your credit report.

Credit Over 62

Under the federal Equal Credit Opportunity Act, a bank or any other institution granting credit or making a loan may not deny credit or terminate existing accounts due to your age. If you are sixty-two years of age or older, you may not be denied credit merely because credit insurance is not available because of your age. Credit insurance pays off your debt if you die or become disabled before your debt has been fully repaid. Lenders or credit card issuers often offer this insurance to you when you take out a loan or a credit card; however, it generally is not a particularly good buy. You can usually do better on your own if you feel a need to buy insurance.

The Equal Credit Opportunity Act also provides protection for people who retire, reach the age of sixty-two, or have a joint account with a spouse who predeceases them. In these instances, the law does not permit the creditor to automatically close or change the terms of the account. However, the creditor is allowed to ask you to update your information or to reapply if the creditor reasonably believes that your income will no longer be sufficient to support the particular line of credit. After you have submitted the new information or have reapplied, the creditor must give you an answer within 30 days. During this time you may continue to use your account without any additional restrictions.

If your new application is rejected, you must be given the specific reasons for the rejection. The Equal Credit Opportunity Act does not assure that you will be granted credit, but at least it does offer some measure of protection.

Good News—Bad News

The good news (if you are 62 or over) is that it is perfectly permissible for a creditor to favor people who are at least 62. The bad news is that a creditor is allowed to consider whether your being close to retirement age may mean that your income will be lower, thereby lowering your creditworthiness.

Optimistic Lenders

I believe my father and mother were well into their 80s when they obtained a twenty-year mortgage through a refinancing of their home. My parents were happy to learn that their bank had such faith in their longevity. However, it is perfectly legal for a bank to consider the age of an applicant as it relates to his or her creditworthiness, such as whether he or she would be expected to live long enough to repay the loan. So an eighty-year-old may legitimately be turned down when applying for a thirty-year mortgage.

Tip *If all your accounts are held jointly with your spouse and you are con-*
cerned that if your spouse dies, you may have difficulty getting credit, you should
open some individual accounts even while your spouse is alive. When you apply
for a credit card in your own name, request that the credit card issuer consider
your spouse's credit report as well as your own in determining your credit
worthiness. This is relevant information if it shows your ability to handle credit;
for example, if you have ever written the checks for payments to an account in
your spouse's name, that helps to demonstrate your creditworthiness.

Who Are You Going to Call?

Ghostbusters—the refrain and answer to the question, "Who are you going
to call?" from the song and movie *Ghostbusters* might help if you are having
trouble with a paranormal oppressor. But if you believe that your rights under
the Equal Credit Opportunity Act have been violated, you can report the
violation for investigation to the appropriate federal agency. To which agency
you report your complaint depends on the type of business with which you were
dealing.

For retail stores, mortgage companies, and credit card companies, you should
file your complaint with the Federal Trade Commission at the following
address:

Consumer Response Center
Federal Trade Commission
600 Pennsylvania Avenue, NW
Washington, D.C. 20580

If your complaint is about a federally chartered bank, you should send your
complaint to the following address:

Comptroller of the Currency
Compliance Management
Mail Stop 7-5
Washington, D.C. 20219

If your complaint is about a state-chartered bank that is insured by the Federal Deposit Insurance Corporation (FDIC), you should send your complaint to the following address:

Federal Deposit Insurance Corporation
Consumer Affairs Division
Washington, D.C. 20429

If you are not sure as to the appropriate agency, you can always send your complaint to the United States Department of Justice at the following address:

Department of Justice
Civil Rights Division
Washington, D.C. 20530

For Love or Money

Husbands and wives today deserve a lot of credit. Sometimes though, heading into a marriage, one spouse may find that his or her credit is better than that of his or her fiancé. And he or she may not want to stain his or her own credit with the bad credit of the other person. Nor does he or she have to do so. Marriage may be a joining together for better or worse, in sickness and in health, but it does not have to be a joining of credit.

First, it should be noted that credit reports are individual matters. When people marry, they do not have a joint credit report and a joint credit score. There is no law requiring married people to have joint accounts or add their spouses to their individual accounts. Often you will find people joining together financially, particularly for big-ticket items, such as buying a house. In that instance, the credit of each may be necessary to qualify for a mortgage loan, and both husband and wife will be responsible for the repayment of the loan and each will have the financial history of that loan reported on his or her individual credit report. You may also, if you choose, add your spouse to your other accounts and in effect provide your credit history to the other person. This may be a way for one spouse who had little or no credit history to instantly gain a credit history because the accounts are reported on the credit report of each person on the account without any indication as to how long someone has been on the account.

Individual Accounts and Joint Accounts

Accounts can either be individual or joint. An individual account, whether you are single or married is, reported on your credit report and not that of your spouse. If you maintain an individual credit card account, for example, your spouse is not held responsible for making payments for charges on the credit card.

Joint accounts are accounts, such as credit cards that may be held in the name of two or more people, such as in the case of a husband and wife. In that case, each of the individuals is responsible for the full payment of the bill to the creditor and each gets the full history of the account reported on his or her own credit report. This can be helpful for someone who wants to establish a credit history, but it can also be detrimental if one person is not making the payments required because that person's financial negligence is reported on the credit report of the other. Although this can harm the credit of the financially responsible person, the law does permit a 100 word explanation to be added to the individual's credit report by which the more financially responsible person can explain the true history of the account.

A third option available is to maintain an individual account but to authorize another person to be able to use the credit, for instance, as an additional sign-er on a credit card account. This arrangement can benefit the spouse added as an authorized user because the history of the account is reported on the cred-it report of the authorized user without the corresponding obligation to make payments on the account.

Credit Following a Divorce

Married people, particularly women, have found themselves at a disadvantage following a divorce if they did not have a significant credit history as reflected on a credit report based upon the marriage's financial history. For this reason, married people should consider both maintaining their own individual accounts as well as using joint accounts or authorized user accounts. This ensures that in the event of a divorce there is a sufficient credit history reflect-ed on her credit report to facilitate access to credit following a divorce.

Tip *If you change your name following a marriage, it is important to make sure that your creditors and the credit reporting bureaus are informed regarding the change of name so that your credit history does not become compromised or lost.*

But what happens to your credit when you divorce? If divorcing people had joint credit accounts, it makes no difference to the creditor who the divorce court judge determines will be responsible for the payment of the account. The creditor is not bound in any way to the judge's determination of the allocation of the payment of credit card debt between the spouses, for example. If the divorcing husband and wife had a joint credit card account prior to the divorce that the judge ordered the husband to pay, and the husband did not make timely payments, the wife's credit rating is adversely affected and the creditor can seek payment in full from her. The wife's only recourse is to go after her former husband in court for contempt of the judge's order.

In the event of a divorce, it is a good idea to close joint accounts; otherwise, each spouse would still be tied financially to the other and still responsible for whatever charges might be run up by the former spouse. Another alternative is to ask the creditor to change the account from a joint account to an individual account. The credit card company or other creditor is not required to honor this request. They may require that you reapply for credit individually and then, based upon that new application, determine either to establish an individual account or deny credit altogether. A creditor may not close a joint account merely because of a divorce, but is permitted by law to close an account at the request of either spouse on the account. The bank holding a mortgage loan, which is most often the joint obligation of the husband and wife, will generally not release one spouse from the debt. This most often necessitates one spouse refinancing the property in his or her own name individually in order to get his or her spouse's name removed from the loan.

11

CREDIT REPORTS

S anta Claus may know if you have been bad or good, at least in the 1934 song "Santa Claus Is Coming to Town" by J. Fred Coots and Henry Gillespie, but I'll bet the jolly old elf does not have as much information about you as the three major credit reporting agencies have in their files. Although your position on the naughty or nice scale may affect what you receive from Santa, your credit report and credit score can affect you much more significantly—from getting a job to getting a mortgage to whether or not an insurance company will do business with you. Often, the first indication you have that you have been victimized by identity theft is on your credit report.

Big Business

According to the Federal Reserve Bulletin of February 2003, the credit reporting system of the three main credit agencies has information on 1.5 billion accounts held by about 190 million people. This information is analyzed by businesses using credit-scoring formulas to decide whether to do business with you and under what terms. And this is a good thing. As Fed Chairman Alan Greenspan said in testimony to the House Financial Services Committee in April 2003, "...there is just no question that unless we have some major sophisticated system of credit evaluation continuously updated, we will have very great difficulty in maintaining the level of consumer credit currently available because clearly, without the information that comes from various credit bureaus and other sources, lenders would have to impose an additional risk premium because of the uncertainty before they make such loans or may, indeed, choose not to make those loans at all. So it is clearly in the interest of consumers to have information continuously flowing into these markets.

It keeps credit available to everybody, including the most marginal buyers. It keeps interest rates lower than they would otherwise be because the uncertainties which would be required otherwise will not be there." And when Alan Greenspan speaks, everyone listens.

How the System Works

Each of the three major credit-reporting agencies receives over two billion items of information on individual accounts monthly that is reported to them voluntarily by businesses with which consumers have accounts. These businesses report positive information about the account, such as a prompt payment history, as well as negative information, such as late payments or the turning of an account over to a collection agency. All this information is organized and used to create individual credit reports for consumers. The information within a person's individual credit report is used to calculate the credit score for that individual. Again, it should be noted that because each of the credit reporting agencies independently assembles its own credit reports on individuals, the credit report and resulting credit score will differ from agency to agency, thereby creating triple the chances of having mistakes on your credit report.

When a consumer applies for credit, the business to which he is applying requests a copy of his credit report from whichever credit-reporting agency it uses in order to evaluate the application. This happens more than two million times a day.

What Is in Your Credit Report?

Your credit report contains the mother-lode of personal information about you. In the hands of the wrong people, you could become the victim of identity theft faster than you can wave a credit card or say Jack Robinson. Why you would want to say "Jack Robinson" is beyond me. Also beyond my understanding is how the saying of the words "faster than you can say Jack Robinson" entered the language as a phrase meaning very quickly. What we do know is that the phrase has been with us since the 1700s, but as to who he was and how his name got to be synonymous with speed, we probably will never know. Personally I think the two syllables "Jack Smith" should be the name by which we measure speed, although somehow I doubt that it will catch on.

Your credit report has your name, address, birth date, Social Security number, place of employment, employment history and your spouse's name. It indicates whether you own a home and where you lived previously. It lists the accounts you have with various creditors, how much credit has been extended to you, and when you paid it back. And if you did not pay it back, it shows whether your bill went to a collection agency or a lawsuit.

Your credit report also indicates who has been asking for your credit report within the past year or as long ago as two years if it was an inquiry related to employment.

Bankruptcies, tax liens, foreclosures, and other public records also find their way to your credit report.

Your credit report is a critical document because the information contained within it and the credit score derived from the information can affect your ability to obtain credit cards, mortgage loans, car loans, insurance policies, or even a job.

Who Has a Right to See Your Credit Report?

Anyone with a "legitimate business need" may obtain a copy of your credit report. Unfortunately, the combination of this being a pretty vague term and the credit reporting agencies not being particularly vigilant in protecting your information has caused numerous situations of people who have no business having your credit report gaining access to it.

Legitimate businesses, such as credit card companies, landlords, and insurance companies routinely view credit reports. Prospective employers may look at your credit report, but generally only with your express permission.

Who Should Not Have Access to Your Credit Report?

Your fiancée's mother. In the 2002 8th U.S. Circuit Court of Appeals case Phillips vs. Grendahl, the court ruled that it was improper for a mother to get the credit report of her prospective son-in-law in order to check him out.

According to the court, "investigating a person because he wants to marry one's daughter" was not a legitimate purpose for obtaining a credit report. This case also highlighted the ease with which people are able to obtain credit reports and how vulnerable we all are to identity theft because of all the personal information contained in credit reports.

How Do I Obtain My Credit Report?

Although you can get copies of your credit reports through companies that will do the work for you, the best advice is to go right to the source. You can obtain a copy from each of the three major credit-reporting agencies directly. Under the provisions of the Fair and Accurate Credit Transactions Act of 2003, you are entitled to a free copy of your credit report annually from each of the three major credit-reporting agencies.

You can contact Equifax at 1-800-685-1111 or www.equifax.com.

You can contact Experian at 1-888-397-3742 or www.experian.com.

You can contact TransUnion at 1-800-916-8800 or www.transunion.com.

Reviewing Your Credit Report

According to a study by the U.S. Public Interest Research Group, 29 percent of credit reports had serious errors that would affect the credit scores of the individuals with the mistaken reports. Due to the fact that each of the three major credit reporting agencies, Equifax, Experian, and TransUnion, independently collects and maintains the information contained in their credit reports, your credit score may differ significantly from credit reporting agency to credit reporting agency.

If you find an error in your credit report, you should notify the credit-reporting agency that you dispute the particular item or items and indicate your reason for doing so. It may be that the information in your report reflects identity theft or someone else's debt may have mistakenly been placed on your report. In any event, after you have informed the credit-reporting agency of the problem, they have no more than 45 days during which to investigate the problem, unless they consider your request to be a frivolous one. If the credit-reporting agency finds in its investigation that the information is indeed inaccurate, the information must be deleted from your file and, at your request, a corrected copy of your report will be sent to anyone who was sent a copy of your mistaken report. If the information in your report is incomplete, the credit reporting agency must make sure the information is accurate and complete. So, for example, if your report shows that you made late payments but neglects to show that you are now up to date in your payments, your report must be corrected to reflect this fact. If, as a result of the investigation, the credit reporting agency is not able to verify one way or the other whether the contested information contained in your report is accurate or not, it must be deleted.

If on the other hand the credit-reporting agency determines that the material contained within your credit report is both accurate and timely, they must notify you of this determination and inform you of your right to have your version of, as Paul Harvey would say, "the rest of the story" added to your credit report. Your statement of explanation may not exceed 100 words.

Free Advice

Combine the fact that mistaken, inaccurate and outdated material may appear on your credit record with the fact that it can take a long time to correct mistakes on a credit report and you have a recipe for disaster. This is particularly true, for example, if you are in the midst of applying for a mortgage loan and your credit score is lower than it should be. When you add to this situation the possibility that your spouse might well be saying "I told you to take care of that a long time ago" and you have ample reason to check out your credit report for accuracy at least six months before applying for a mortgage loan.

A Million Dollar Mistake

In 1996, Judy Thomas first became aware that her credit report contained notations of a large number of accounts that did not belong to her. In addition, she noticed that her credit report identified her as "Judy Thomas, aka Judith Upton." No fraud or identity theft was involved. The mistake of adding information about Judith Upton's credit report to the credit report of Judy Thomas was probably made because the women both shared a similar first name, the same year of birth, and, perhaps most significantly, Social Security numbers that differed by only a single digit.

Upon becoming aware of the mistaken information contained in her credit report, Judy Thomas notified TransUnion, the credit-reporting agency whose credit report on her reflected this improper information, and requested that the false information be deleted from her credit report. TransUnion did delete some of the mistaken information but left most of it intact after it reportedly verified the information with the creditors that provided the initial information to TransUnion. The reason for this became apparent later when it was learned that credit-reporting agencies, at that time, usually verified accounts by merely inquiring of the creditor as to whether the particular information was the same information that previously had been reported by the creditor to the credit-reporting agency. Obviously, this is not a good way to verify the accuracy of mistakenly provided information. What would have been a more effective way to verify the accuracy of the information would have been to supply the creditors with all the information that Judy Thomas had independently gathered and provided to TransUnion to indicate that the challenged accounts were indeed not her accounts.

In 1999, Judy Thomas applied for a mortgage and was denied because of the tainted accounts of Judith Upton that remained on Judy Thomas' credit report. To make things even worse, the few accounts of Judith Upton's that had been removed earlier from Judy Thomas' credit report reappeared on Judy Thomas' credit report. Taking matters into her own hands, Judy Thomas contacted the creditors directly and even was aided by the real Judith Upton who agreed with Judy Thomas that the questionable accounts were indeed her accounts and not Judy Thomass'. Despite Judy Thomas's best efforts, TransUnion still identified Judy Thomas as "aka Judith Upton" until December 2001. Eventually she sued TransUnion, alleging that it had been negligent in permitting the mistakes on her credit report to occur and in failing to correct them. After a trial that lasted a week, the jury came back with a verdict in her favor, ordering TransUnion to pay her $300,000 in compensatory damages and then added five million dollars of punitive damages to the verdict, declaring that the actions of TransUnion were "willful." The punitive damage amount was later reduced on appeal to a still pretty substantial one million dollars.

Another Scary Story

In March 2000, when Lorraine Turner found her 1993 Chevrolet Geo Prism was missing she reported the theft to the police. In doing so, she learned the car had not been stolen, but had been repossessed due to her failure to make her car payments. There was only one problem with that explanation. Not only had Ms. Turner been up to date in her car loan payments, she had even completed her payments in full some time ago. She also had in her possession the title to the car, which had, weeks earlier, been returned to her by the bank where she had her car loan. Her car was promptly returned to her and Lorraine Turner thought the incident was over. But she was wrong. Three years later when she went to buy a new car she was turned down for a car loan because her credit report reflected the wrongful repossession of her 1993 Chevrolet Geo Prism. Her efforts to have the bank correct the situation were futile, so she sued the bank for its continuous inaccurate reporting of her car's repossession and failure to correct the credit report error caused by their negligence. A sympathetic jury ruled in her favor and awarded her $500,000. Now she can pay cash for her next car.

Credit Scoring

If Grantland Rice was right and it isn't important whether you win or lose, why do they keep score? Let's face it; whether it is a student's SAT score, the Red Sox-Yankee score, or your credit score that can determine whether you are extended credit and at what rate, scoring is important. Your credit score, as contained on your credit report, is of particular importance.

If You Can't Beat Them, Join Them

I've Got a Secret was the name of a popular television quiz show from years ago. It also, until recently, could have described the manner of doing business of Fair Isaac & Co., a business whose creditworthiness scores are used by companies throughout the business world in determining whether or not to grant credit to applicants. Beginning in the 1950s, a number of companies, the most prominent of which is Fair Isaac, have used complex formulas to analyze the information contained in individual credit reporting agency files to arrive at a number or score that evaluates a person's creditworthiness. For years,

Fair Isaac protected its secret formula for credit scoring believing that if people knew how credit scoring was done, they would try to manipulate the system. In 2001, Fair Isaac decided that it would disclose a full list of the factors that go into the score and the statistical weight that it gives each element. They beat the California legislature to the punch—it was about to pass a law requiring Fair Isaac to make their scoring system public. These scores that are called FICO scores have been used not just for mortgage applications, but also for other consumer loans and credit card application evaluations. Armed with this information, consumers can now see how their actions affect their credit.

Do You Want to Know a Secret?

Just like KFC carefully guards Colonel Sanders's secret recipe of 11 herbs and spices, so does Fair Isaac still carefully guard the precise calculations of how its credit scoring system works, although they have released broad guidelines. However, leaks occur. As my grandmother used to say, "I can keep a secret, it is the people I tell it to that can't keep a secret." And just as leaks have occurred regarding the Colonel's secret formula for fried chicken (it is alleged to involve rosemary, oregano, sage, ginger, marjoram, thyme, brown sugar, pepper, paprika, garlic, and onion according to www.recipegoldmine.com), so have leaks occurred about how FICO computes credit scores. In addition, Fair Isaac itself has joined the parade and supplies some telling information on its own.

The No-Longer Secret Formula

Under the now disclosed broad outline of the FICO formula, your record of timely payments of loans accounts for 35% of your FICO score; the amount and type of outstanding debt that you have accounts for 30% of your score; the length of your credit history, 15% of your score; the mix of your various credit accounts, 10% of your score; and finally, the number and types of accounts that you have opened recently makes up the remaining 10% of your score.

What's Your Score?

For many people, "What's your score?" has become a more popular phrase than "What's your sign?" although it will never be much of a pick-up line in a bar. It will, however, affect your life much more than your horoscope will. Your ability to get a car loan or a mortgage loan is affected by your credit score. How low an interest rate you will get on your loan is affected by your credit score. Many people are unaware that their credit scores may have resulted in their paying a higher interest rate on their mortgage loans than if they had a higher credit score. Telephone companies also use credit scores to determine whether to provide service and, if so, what deposit they may require. Your credit score may also affect how much you may be authorized to take out on a daily basis from your bank's ATM. Even when you apply for a job, your credit score is important. Some prospective employers equate bad credit with unreliability, regardless of your astrological sign.

FICO credit scores range between 300 and 850. As so often is the case (with the notable exception of your cholesterol reading), the higher your score, the better. If your credit score is over 660, Freddie Mac, a company that plays an important role in the mortgage market, considers your credit score to be high enough so that you will be approved for most mortgage loans with only a basic review of your application. If your score is between 620 and 660, your score is more problematic and a more detailed review of your application will be required. A score of less than 620 results in a difficult time getting mortgage financing. A score of 666 may affect your credit in ways you can hardly imagine, particularly if you share the surname of Buffalo Sabres' professional hockey player Miroslav Satan, who of course places the emphasis on the second syllable of his name when pronouncing it. Scores above 770 can often work to your benefit as to the terms of your loan, such as a lower interest rate.

In most states, whether you will be granted an insurance policy and at what cost is affected by your credit score, although there is a welcome trend among the states to limit the use of credit reports by companies selling homeowner's insurance and car insurance. For years, insurance companies have argued that, according to their secret formulas, a person's credit score has a direct relationship to the number of claims that they make on their insurance. Consumer advocates have responded by saying that this practice is spurious (a great word that is derived from the Latin word "spurius," meaning illegitimate or false) and discriminatory, particularly against poor people and minorities. The use of credit reports in making employment decisions has also come under fire as being discrimination. Brenda Matthews, an African-American, had her job offer from Johnson & Johnson rescinded after the company reviewed her credit report. Brenda Matthews's lawyers say that African-Americans have historically been discriminated against in the credit market and that this is reflected in their credit reports. The Equal Employment Opportunity Commission has previously ruled that in some circumstances failing to hire someone because of poor credit may be considered illegal discrimination, but that each case must be judged on its individual facts. According to the Federal Trade Commission, in order to justify a company policy of evaluating a job candidate through his or her credit report, the company must show that creditworthiness relates somehow to the job, as well as being consistent with business necessity. Proponents of using credit history for hiring purposes argue that an applicant with a great deal of debt is more likely to steal.

What Does Not Affect Your FICO Score?

Your FICO score does not consider your age, your race, sex, marital status, job, or where you live. Your FICO score also does not consider the fact that you may be using the services of a credit counselor either for you or against you in determining your score. For years, there had been a concern that the constructive step of working with a credit counselor to improve your spending and credit habits would actually be used against you when you applied for credit.

How Often Is Your FICO Score Updated?

Your FICO score is regularly updated and recalculated using the latest information that comes into the credit reporting agencies. Because that information is just a bit different every time your file is looked at, your score will fluctuate as well.

State Scoring

According to a study done by Experian, the credit-reporting agency, the state with the lowest average credit score is Texas with an average score of 653. The state with the highest average score was North Dakota, although its small population may affect the state's high average score. North Dakota ranks forty-seventh of all the states in population, thereby putting a lot of pressure on individual North Dakotans to maintain their good credit ratings to ensure state bragging rights. The national average credit score was 678. The Experian scores, which it calls PLUS scores, are similar to but not identical to the FICO scores.

Timeliness

Not surprisingly, in calculating your credit score, being 30 days late is worse than being 90 days late. However a 30 day late payment that occurred within the last month will hurt your score more than a single 90 day late payment from six years ago. And believe it or not, according to Fair Isaac, between 60 percent and 65 percent of all credit reports contain no late payments.

Tip *When settling an overdue bill, make a condition of any settlement you make with your creditor that it request that the credit reporting agency remove any negative remarks about your account and instead report the debt as having been paid satisfactorily or paid as agreed. This will help your credit score.*

Your Credit Limit

Generally, the better your credit, the higher the credit limit a credit card company will offer you. After all, if you are a good credit risk, the more you use your credit card the more money the credit card company makes off of you as a customer.

Sometimes you can get an increased credit limit merely by asking your credit card company for it. And sometimes you don't even have to ask for an increase because just like Santa Claus is always watching to see who are the good girls and boys, so are the credit card companies constantly monitoring your credit card activity. If you have shown that you are handling your credit well, you may receive a notice from your credit card company raising your credit limit without you even asking. It is important to remember that just because your credit card company asked you to the prom, you do not have to go with them. If you have concerns about your ability to handle credit, just say no; or if you are feeling particularly polite, "No, thank you." You are under no obligation to accept an increase in your credit line. For many of us, however, turning down an increased credit limit is difficult. We find ourselves much like Oscar Wilde who said, "I can resist anything except temptation." But try.

Why Would You Refuse a Credit Line Increase?

Although at first blush, it would appear that there is no harm in accepting a large increase in your credit line if you have the discipline to use it (or refrain from using it) wisely, there are other reasons to consider refusing an increase in your credit line. Your ability to obtain a car loan or a mortgage could actually be adversely affected by having credit cards with exceptionally high credit lines. This is because when a lender looks at your open credit lines, it focuses on your ability to quickly and easily run up your debts, which can affect their decision to lend you money. As the great financial philosopher Dirty Harry Callahan said in the movie *Magnum Force*, "A man's got to know his limitations."

Timing Is Everything

It would seem to make sense to cancel any of your credit cards with large credit limits that you do not use. However, taking that step could actually harm your credit score. To understand this seemingly contradictory proposition, we need to do a little math. One of the factors in determining your credit score is the total amount of debt that you carry on your credit cards divided by the total amount of your available credit lines on those cards. If the result of that computation is 1, you are in trouble because it means you have borrowed to your utmost limit—not a good sign. Using this formula, the lower the resulting fraction, the better your credit score. So, for example, if you were carrying $5,000 of debt on five credit cards with total available credit lines of $20,000, you are using one-fourth of your available credit. If, however, you canceled a credit card that you did not use anyway that carried a credit limit of $5,000, you would now be using one-third of your available credit and your credit score would be adversely affected.

Credit History

In determining your credit history for credit score purposes, the age of your oldest account as well as the age of all your accounts are both considered. They also look at the age of specific accounts and how long it may have been since those accounts were active.

Fair Isaac recommends that people only recently establishing credit should be cognizant of the fact that opening a large number of new accounts in a short period of time will lower the average age of your accounts, which can lower your credit score.

Don't Know Much About History

Sam Cook first sang about not knowing much about history, and Simon and Garfunkel were apparently aware of history because they sang the same song, "Wonderful World" years later and also had a hit record with it. But if your credit score is hurting because it does not show enough of your financial history, there are things you can do about it. First of all, get your report and see if it is missing things that could add to your credit history and improve your score. Under the Fair and Accurate Credit Transaction Act of 2003, everyone has the right to a free credit report from each of the three major credit-reporting agencies. Not all your financial dealings are automatically reported to the credit reporting bureaus and added to your credit report from which is derived your credit score. If you have creditors whom you have been paying on a regular basis, ask them to report this fact to the credit reporting agencies.

Establishing a Credit History Quickly

An apparent paradox in getting credit is that unless you have already have a history of good credit, it can be hard to get credit. So how do you make history? Ask a friend or relative (or best of all, a friendly relative) with good credit to apply as a co-signer with you for a credit card. This makes it easier to obtain a credit card if you lack a sufficient credit history to get a credit card on your own. After you have established your own credit history through the responsible use of the credit card, you can then apply for a credit card on your own and cancel the card you got with the friendly co-signer.

Secured Credit Cards

If you are unable to get a conventional credit card and want to establish credit, get a secured credit card. They are easy to get and if, over time, you are able to show that you can handle the secured credit card responsibly, you will find that your credit score will improve, and you will likely be able to get a regular credit card. In fact, FICO scores cannot be calculated unless you have a minimum of one account that has been open for at least six months. Through the responsible use of a secured credit card, you can take a first step toward a good credit score. A secured credit card looks just like a regular Visa or MasterCard credit card. The issuing bank requires you to deposit a sum of money to secure your credit limit. With a secured credit card, the bank has little risk and you get the ability to establish your creditworthiness. As always, shop around for the best deal with the least fees. Again, www.bankrate.com is a good place to go to compare various secured credit cards.

Tip *Many of us are inundated with offers to get a new credit card and consolidate our debt from other cards by paying off the other cards with checks from the new card and transferring the old credit card debt to the new card. This maneuver is always fraught with fine print traps, although in some circumstances it may make sense. However, it is also important to consider that as far as your credit score is considered, when you close long held credit cards, you reduce your credit history, which can, in turn, lower your credit score.*

Credit Inquiries

If you decide that you need another credit card (Americans today have an average of 3.2 cards per person), you should think twice before filling out a bunch of applications for new credit cards. When you apply for a credit card, the credit card company looks at your credit report. This is called a "hard inquiry," and it can adversely affect your credit score if you have a lot of hard inquiries. It affects your credit score because it indicates you are considering taking on a large amount of additional credit that could affect your ability to meet your financial obligations if you ran up your credit limits.

Just as Johnny Lee warned us in the song "Lookin' for Love in All the Wrong Places" in the movie *Urban Cowboy*, so can you hurt your credit score by looking for credit in too many places. Applying for a lot of credit and incurring "hard inquiries" can reduce your credit score.

Soft inquiries occur when either you or one of your already existing creditors checks out your credit report. Soft inquiries will not affect your credit score in any way.

When shopping for a mortgage or a car loan, it is a good thing to do a bit of comparison-shopping. However, if in so doing, the lenders you contact each check out your credit report, the rash of inquiries can actually hurt your credit score and work against your getting favorable mortgage terms. The solution is to compare rates informally before narrowing your choice of potential lenders.

ᴥ Loophole

All three of the major credit-reporting agencies look at automobile loan and mortgage loan inquiries within a 14 day period as only counting as a single inquiry for purposes of your credit score so you can do a little comparison shopping without being too fearful of lowering your credit score. In addition, your credit score is not affected by inquiries done in the 30 days before your score is calculated, which means that if you complete your loan shopping within 30 days, your loan shopping will not lower your score.

A Healthy Diet

Just as a good mix of fruits, whole grains, and vegetables contribute to a healthy diet, so does a healthy mix of different types of credit contribute to a healthy credit score. A proper combination of credit card accounts, retail store accounts, automobile and other installment loans, and mortgage loans can help show that you can handle different types of credit. This does not mean, however, that you should open new credit accounts just to improve the mix of your credit.

Retail Credit Cards

It is not uncommon when you are shopping at a particular retail store, such as Sears, to be told that if you sign up for their own credit card, you can get an immediate discount of usually around ten percent on your purchase. What could be the harm in doing so? Anytime you open a new account, a credit inquiry is added to your credit report. Because credit inquiries can lower your credit score that simple transaction could contribute to a lower credit score that in turn could contribute to a higher mortgage rate. In addition, adding another credit card to your stable of credit cards lowers the average age of your credit history, which lowers your overall credit score. So if you are going to use that card on a regular basis, it may make sense to open a retail credit card account, but if the retailer accepts the credit cards that you already have, the advantage of having a store credit card may be minimal at best.

No Good Deed Goes Unpunished

Negative information on your credit report such as an unpaid account is automatically removed from your credit report after seven years. But what if you have an account that is six years old that shows up as having gone to collection on your credit report? Logically, it would seem that if you made a payment on that account, it would be helpful to your credit. Unfortunately logic does not always play a role in the world of credit reports and credit scoring. By making a payment on that overdue account in collection, you will have transformed the account from an old account that is about to disappear from your credit report in another year to a current collection account that will stay on your credit report for many more years. Perhaps the best action to take is to get your creditor to agree, in return for your payment, to report the account to the credit reporting agencies as being satisfactorily paid in return for your payment rather than being designated as a current collection account.

Closed Accounts

Even if you close an account, that account will appear on your credit report and contribute toward the calculation of your credit score. Negative account information must be removed from your account after seven years. Bankruptcies, however, are an exception to that rule; they remain on your credit report for ten years.

Canceling a Credit Card

Perhaps you are looking to take the advice of Henry David Thoreau to "Simplify, simplify, simplify" by closing some credit cards in an effort to reduce your risk of identity theft as well as remove a bit of temptation. If so, which cards should you close?

Close accounts with small credit limits. The effect on your credit score will be minimal. Close retail store cards. You don't need them. Close more recently obtained credit cards. The longer your credit history, the better your score.

There is a right way and a wrong way to cancel a credit card. First and foremost, do not cancel a card while you still have an outstanding balance owed on the card. Some credit card issuers have provisions buried within the fine print of their contracts that allow them to raise your interest rate to astronomical levels in that event. Wait until you have fully paid off the card before you start the cancellation procedure. And make it easier on yourself by not using the card when you intend to cancel it in the not too distant future.

After you have fully paid off the balance on the credit card, contact the card issuer by telephone and tell them that you are canceling the card. You can reach them at the customer service telephone number imprinted on the back of your credit card. Be prepared to spend a lot of time on the phone as they bounce you from person to person who will try to talk you out of canceling the card. They may try to entice you to stay by offering better terms than you presently have. They may offer a lower interest rate, a reduction in fees, or other inducements to stay. It is most important that you remind them to report the cancellation of your card to the credit reporting bureaus as "closed at customer's request." This is crucial because if the account is reported to the credit reporting bureaus as "closed by creditor," your credit score will suffer.

Follow up your telephone conversation with the customer service representative with a letter that you send to the card issuer by certified mail confirming your cancellation of the card and your request that they notify the credit-reporting bureau that the account was closed at your request.

Wait about a month and then check your credit report to make sure that the account is shown as closed at your request. If a mistake has occurred and the account is shown as being closed by the creditor, contact the customer service department again and report the mistake. Follow up your conversation with them with another letter sent by certified mail and make sure that you include a copy of your first letter with the second letter.

The Battle Against Aging

The lines that some people think of when they think about the battle against aging is often the lines on their faces; however, it may be more productive to think about the aging of credit lines.

The concept of re-aging of overdue accounts is largely unknown to many people who could be helped greatly by this process that is specifically author-ized by the Federal Financial Institutions Examination Council (FFIEC), a part of the Federal Reserve.

Re-aging is the name for the process by which your creditor, such as a credit card company with which you may be behind in your payments, agrees to for-give your being late and reclassify your account as up to date. This does not mean that your debt is in any way reduced, but it does stop further late fees and it does greatly enhance your credit report and correspondingly, your cred-it score.

How Many Psychiatrists Does It Take to Change a Light Bulb?

How many psychiatrists does it take to change a light bulb? Only one, but the light bulb has to demonstrate a sincere desire to change.

In order to qualify for re-aging of your credit card account, the standards established by the FFIEC state that the credit card issuer must establish and follow a policy that requires the consumer to demonstrate a renewed willingness and ability to repay the debt. A further condition to qualify for re-aging is that the account be at least nine months old and the borrower must make at least three consecutive minimum monthly payments or a payment equal to that amount.

Sounds pretty good, eh? But before you rush to your credit card issuer to request re-aging of a delinquent account, you should be aware that there are other conditions imposed by the FFIEC. According to the FFIEC, accounts should not be re-aged more than once within a twelve-month period and no more than twice during a five-year period. In addition, it is important to note that these rules established by the FFIEC are only minimum standards. Credit card issuers and other financial institutions are free to enact their own more stringent standards, such as permitting re-aging to be done by a consumer only once. However, particularly if the cause of your financial troubles was temporary in nature, such as a medical problem or a job loss, re-aging just might be the way to go, but first you must convince the credit card issuer to agree to your re-aging plan. As always, make sure you get it in writing if they agree to re-age your account.

How Do I Get My Credit Score?

To paraphrase the theme song from the old sitcom about a talking horse, *Mister Ed*, you can go right to the source and ask the horse. In this case, the source is Fair Isaac itself. Go online to www.myfico.com and you can purchase your score for each of the three major credit-reporting bureaus. Remember, because the three major credit reporting bureaus maintain independent records, your report will most likely differ from agency to agency so it is important to look at your scores from all three credit-reporting agencies. For a free approximation of your credit scores you can go to www.eloan.com.

What Does It All Mean?

When your credit score is generated, a list of as many as four reasons describing why the score was not higher is also produced and will be made available to you. This can be particularly helpful if you were denied credit or received a less advantageous interest rate as a result of a less than stellar credit score. This can also be a good opportunity to find out if you are a victim of identity theft, and it can provide concrete information as to what significantly reduced your score and what you need to do to improve your score. Now that the credit score genie is out of the bottle, FICO and many of the credit card companies have tripped over themselves trying to court consumers as well as make a buck out of consumers' thirst for their credit scores.

Garbage In—Garbage Out

A credit score is only as good as the information used to compute the score. The information used to compute your score is contained in your credit report. Unfortunately, that information can be quite often incorrect due to mistakes, negligence or identity theft. And when harmful incorrect information appears on your credit report, you pay the price. You should regularly monitor your credit report and make the credit-reporting agencies correct any mistakes or identity theft that may appear on your report. Removing inaccurate information from your credit report can be a time consuming matter so it is important not to wait until you are applying for a loan to check out your credit report.

What Can You Do to Improve Your Score?

1. It seems pretty simple, but it is worth saying. Pay your bills on time. If a creditor is looking for a good predictor as to whether or not you will pay your bills in the future, back to the past is not a bad place to go.

2. Reduce your debt. The amount that you owe, particularly as it relates to the credit lines on your credit cards, is an important factor.

3. Keep on keeping on. The longer you have a good credit history, the better. This can work to the detriment of younger people; however, they may be able to make up for this in other ways.

12

CREDIT COUNSELING AND CREDIT REPAIR

I f you're armed with your credit cards and screaming "Charge!" more often than in the battle scenes of *The Lord of the Rings*, you may find that while it is a relatively simple matter to get into debt problems by yourself, sometimes it is helpful to have the assistance of others in resolving these problems. If you find that you are in need of debt counseling, you are not alone. Debt counseling has become a seven billion-dollar industry. Debt counseling can be very helpful if your credit cards have gotten the best of you.

How Bad Is It?

How do you stop an elephant from charging? Take away his credit cards. Elephant jokes are old news, but our addiction to credit card debt in this country goes on and on. Just how bad is our addiction to credit cards? According to the American Bankruptcy Institute (www.abiworld.org), our national credit card debt is around $735 billion dollars, which is an average of almost $7,000 per household.

Credit Counseling Agencies (CCAs)

Sometimes a credit counseling agency is able to negotiate a plan with your creditors through which your creditors will agree to accept reduced payments. A credit counseling agency also may be able to persuade your creditors to agree to reduce your finance charges or waive late fees. Often, the way credit counseling agencies work is that you pay them a single amount each month that they distribute on your behalf to your various creditors in accordance with the plan established by them with your creditors. Such a plan can take anywhere from a year to four years to pay off your creditors. If it takes longer than four years to pay off your creditors, you may be better off considering bankruptcy. Some credit counseling agencies charge you little or nothing for their services while others may charge monthly maintenance fees. Many credit counseling agencies are actually partially funded by contributions from the credit card companies and other creditors.

"I Have Always Depended on the Kindness of Strangers"

Those were the words spoken by the character of Blanche DuBois in Tennessee Williams's classic play, *A Streetcar Named Desire*. It also could apply to how the credit counseling industry worked at the time of its inception during the 1960s. Most of the original credit counseling agencies were part of the National Foundation for Credit Counseling (NFCC). They were local non-profit organizations through which trained counselors provided financial education and advice on how to deal with debt problems as well as information about personal budgeting in order to help avoid those problems in the future.

They also introduced the concept of the "debt management plan," or DMP, through which the client of the credit counseling agency hired the agency to contact their creditors, such as credit card companies, and negotiate a lower monthly payment, lower interest rates, or the waiver of outstanding late fees. The consumer's debts were then lumped into a single monthly payment that the consumer would make to the credit counseling agency which would, in turn, make the agreed upon individual monthly payments to each of the creditors. In return for setting up and managing this arrangement, the credit counseling agency would receive from the creditor a payment known as a "fair share" payment that was used to pay for the cost of operating the non-profit credit counseling agency.

Originally, the fair share payments averaged between 12 and 15 percent of the payments paid to the creditor through the debt management plan. This was the proverbial win-win situation whereby the credit card companies were able to fund an industry that would help the credit card companies receive a larger portion of the credit card debt owed to them than if consumers had gone into bankruptcy or if the debts otherwise became uncollectible. The non-profit credit counseling agencies were thus able to maintain themselves through these fair share payments that allowed them to charge nothing or the most nominal of costs to their customers in order to stay in business. As for consumers, they were aided in not only paying their bills, but in developing the knowledge and discipline required to avoid debt problems in the future. To this day, the fees for member agencies of the NFCC remain low. According to the NFCC 2002 Member Activity Report, the average fee for arranging a debt management plan with a NFCC member agency in 2002 was only $23.09 and the monthly maintenance fee a mere $14.

Effect on Your Credit

Although paying off your debts is a good thing to do for your credit, it is important to remember that debt problems stay on your credit report for seven years. Bankruptcies remain on a credit report for ten years and diamonds are forever. Diamonds will not appear on your credit report, nor will you find any smiley faces on your credit report, however if you are looking for a good James Bond movie to rent, *Diamonds Are Forever* fits the bill. It stars Sean Connery, the real James Bond. Negative information on your credit report, such as late payments or bankruptcies, may make it more difficult to obtain credit in the short term, however eventually as time goes by (which reminds me, you may want to rent *Casablanca*, too) and you make timely payments to your creditors, your credit score will improve.

Consumer Credit Counseling Services

The National Foundation for Credit Counseling has been helping people with debt and credit problems for more than 50 years. Their non-profit affiliates are commonly known as the Consumer Credit Counseling Services and can be found almost anywhere in the country. Counseling is available to people who are in over the heads with debt through face-to-face meetings, phone consultations, or online assistance. Generally, their services are provided at low cost or even at no cost to people with debt problems. The primary source of funding for these agencies comes from the creditors themselves through their "fair share" contributions to the organizations. A good credit counseling agency will take the time to review your financial situation and analyze how you got into debt problems in the first place. They will then make recommendations that may include setting up a budget. The recommended plan may or may not include a debt consolidation program supervised by the credit counseling company through which they may negotiate new terms for the repayment of your debts and coordinate the monthly payments to your creditors. If done properly, your payments to individual creditors can be reduced.

Credit Repair Scams

Despite what you may be told by some credit repair services, information that is verifiably correct cannot be removed from your credit report. However, if you find incorrect information on your credit report you may request the credit reporting service to investigate the item and remove it if is either shown to be incorrect or even if it merely cannot be verified. The Federal Trade Commission has recently been cracking down on illegitimate credit repair companies. In a case brought by the U.S. Attorney for the Western District of Texas, Clifton W. Cross was not only ordered to pay $175,000 in restitution to defrauded customers, but was also sentenced to 49 months in federal prison. Clifton Cross, through his company Build-It-Fast, used a Web site to entice customers to hire him to demonstrate how they could erase their old bad credit and obtain a new clean credit report. At the crux of the scheme was a common technique known as file segregation. Cross sold instructions to customers that informed them how they could obtain an Employer Identification Number from the IRS and use it to achieve file segregation and set up a new credit history for themselves free of all the harmful information contained in their former credit reports. Properly used, an employer identification number identifies employers, trusts, and other entities for tax purposes. It has the same number of digits as a Social Security number. Unfortunately for the people buying into this scam, using file segregation to change your credit history is a felony. In addition, advising consumers as to how they can hide their true credit histories is a violation of the Federal Credit Repair Organizations Act. The temptation to fall for the claims of these fraudulent credit repair companies is easy to understand. Wary consumers should always remember that any credit repair service that says that it can get rid of accurate harmful credit information from your credit report earlier than seven years from the time it first occurred is just too good to be true.

Promises to Keep

In his lovely poem "Stopping by Woods on a Snowy Evening" Robert Frost spoke of "...promises to keep and miles to go before I sleep." Unfortunately, there are many unscrupulous credit repair services that will make many promises to you, but they will not be able to legally keep those promises and you will end up being the one losing sleep. They will promise you that regardless of your credit history, they can immediately clean it up, get rid of accurate (but negative) information on your credit report, and put you in a position to obtain credit, a car loan, a mortgage or insurance.

Things to Watch Out For

1. They want a big up-front payment before they do anything for you. According to the Federal Credit Repair Organizations Act that has been in effect since 1997, you are not required to pay a credit repair service until its work has been completed.

2. They recommend that you establish a new clean credit report by applying for an Employer Identification Number, using IRS Form SS-4, to use as your identifying number instead of your Social Security number, which is already associated with your tainted credit report. This misleading tactic is illegal and should be an immediate tip-off that you are dealing with an unscrupulous credit counselor.

3. Where is your first payment to the credit counseling service going? In the fine print, you may find that the first monthly payment of your personal plan goes to the credit counseling service rather than to your creditors. This can harm your credit further.

4. The law requires that any credit repair company give you a copy of "Consumer Credit File Rights Under State and Federal Law" before you sign any contract for its services. It is important to read this before hiring any credit repair company in order to learn what they can and cannot do for you as well as to see what you can do for yourself.

5. Read the contract. The law requires that any company that performs credit repair services must have a written contract with you. This contract has to include details as to what the cost will be for its services, what services will be performed on your behalf, how long it will take to

complete its work, and what guarantees it offers. The contract must also specifically state the company's name and address. If you are not offered a written contract or the contract you are offered omits any of this required information, head for the door.

> ### ❧ Loophole
>
> **The Federal Credit Repair Organizations Act provides that a credit repair company shall not do anything on your behalf until three days after you have signed the required written contract with them. During this three-day waiting period you may cancel the contract for any reason and without any penalty.**

How You Can Get into Trouble: Or, If It Looks Too Good to Be True, It Probably Is

We should trust our instincts, but unfortunately desperate people with debt and credit problems all too often look for a quick and easy fix to their problems. It is for that very reason that they are such easy targets for the conmen selling fraudulent and illegal credit repair services. Does anyone really think that there are companies out there with secret methods to instantly cure bad credit?

But just what are the potential consequences if you follow the bad advice of these con artists? If you misrepresent your Social Security number on a loan or credit application, you have committed a federal crime. If you get an Employer Identification Number from the IRS under false pretenses to use for file segregation purposes, you have committed a federal crime. If you provide false information when applying for credit by telephone or mail, you have committed a federal crime. Are you starting to notice a pattern here?

Spam and Credit Repair

Spam, spam, spam formed the basis of a funny Monty Python sketch with which some of you may be familiar. Although spam, when parodied by Monty Python, can be quite funny, spam when it represents junk e-mail flooding your computer can actually get you into trouble. E-mail messages promising to wipe out bankruptcies from your credit history or erase bad credit are quite common. These promises are empty at best and often are involved with the illegal file separation tactic outlawed by the Federal Credit Repair Organizations Act. The Federal Trade Commission, as well as a number of states' attorneys general have taken action against hundreds of Web sites touting these phony credit repair plans that often charge as much as a $1,000 to sell you an illegal plan.

Watch Out for That Helping Hand

The large increase in people having problems handling credit and their resulting debt problems has prompted a rise in the number of companies offering to help debtors solve their debt and credit problems. Bad credit is good business for many of these companies. Unfortunately, not all these companies are legitimate. Their names may sound trustworthy and their ads may look and sound nice, but all too often these companies just are preying upon desperate consumers. The combination of high-pressure sales tactics and misleading advertising can often work against debt-ridden consumers. Sometimes their one-size-fits-all solution is a large debt consolidation loan that they arrange and ends up not helping you a great deal, but does a lot for the wallets of those people who said they were there to help you. And the worst of these companies merely take your money up front and then simply vanish.

Non-Profit for Whom?

Some of the most abusive credit counseling companies have non-profit, tax-exempt status. Generally, when people see that they are dealing with a non-profit organization, they assume that the company is legitimate. And often they are right. The National Foundation for Credit Counseling and its affiliated Consumer Credit Counseling Services are absolutely legitimate sources of credit counseling. However, some other companies call themselves non-profit but charge big fees for their services while they pay their executives salaries of as much as a half a million dollars per year. The Federal Trade Commission, the Internal Revenue Service, as well as various state regulators have all issued consumer alerts in regard to certain tax exempt, non-profit companies offering credit counseling or credit repair services. Many of these fraudulent companies utilize non-profit status not only to make themselves appear more legitimate, but also because some state and federal consumer protection laws do not apply to non-profit, tax exempt organizations.

In its investigation of abuse of non-profit, tax exempt status by deceptive credit counseling companies, the IRS has focused its attention on the requirement that a credit counseling organization must limit its services to poor customers or primarily provide education and counseling to the public in order to legitimately claim non-profit, tax-exempt status. The IRS is also looking at the large salaries paid to some executives at certain credit counseling organizations and the connection between the owners of non-profit credit counseling services and for-profit companies that may be funneled business from the non-profit company. For example, the IRS is looking for situations where the non-profit credit counseling organization uses a for-profit loan company to write debt consolidation loans for its customers.

Howard Beales, Director of the FTC's Bureau of Consumer Protection, recognized that many, if not most, credit counseling agencies operate honestly and fairly. However, he stated though that "The Commission is concerned, however, that some firms may be deceiving consumers about who they are, what they do and how much they charge. The victims of the deception may find themselves in even more dire straits than before."

Because That Is Where the Money Is

The response attributed to famed bank robber Willie Sutton to the question, "Why do you rob banks?" was "Because that is where the money is." When credit card debt began to soar in the 1990s, the number of credit counseling agencies began to soar as well. According to IRS Commissioner Mark Everson, between the years 1994 and 2003 the number of credit counseling agencies applying to the IRS for tax-exempt status was 1,215. And of this number, more than 810 applied for tax-exempt status between the years 2000 and 2003. Unlike the model for the credit counseling agencies of the 1960s, many of these new credit counseling agencies offered little counseling, but instead focused, sometimes exclusively, on debt management programs. Due to the fact that most states required credit counseling companies to be non-profit companies, many of these newer credit counseling agencies were part of a Byzantine connection of for-profit companies with non-profit companies in an attempt to skirt the law while making a substantial buck in the world of credit counseling.

According to the United States Senate Permanent Subcommittee on Investigations Report, "Profiteering in a Non-Profit Industry: Abusive Practices in Credit Counseling" issued on March 24, 2004, the model for the traditional consumer credit counseling agency was "a community-based, modest operation with minimal overhead and expenses. There were no large fees, no large executive salaries, high-priced advertising blitzes, or expensive marketing campaigns. Face-to-face meetings between consumers and credit counselors that last(ed), in some cases, several hours characterized their day-to-day operations. If a consumer enrolled in a DMP, the employees of the CCA would negotiate with the consumer's various creditors, set up the plan, and distribute payments to the creditors until the consumer's debts were paid in full. The traditional CCA did not 'outsource' any of its essential functions to for-profit companies, and millions of dollars did not flow through the CCA to for-profit companies." [1]

In contrast, the report went on to say, "The characteristics of the 'new' CCA model has modified or even reversed the practices of the traditional CCA. The new model is characterized by high consumer fees and lucrative contracts that benefit related for-profit companies. The revenue generated through DMPs is seldom spent on improving or expanding education or counseling, but rather on advertising, marketing, and other activities unrelated to assisting consumers with their financial problems.

The DebtWorks-Ballenger Group Conglomerate

One of the debt management programs that was a focus of the Committee's attention was that of the DebtWorks-Ballenger Group conglomerate, a complicated organization of eleven non profit consumer credit counseling agencies whose debt management programs were serviced by a for-profit company With figures that would make Willie Sutton envious, the total amount of consumer debt managed by these companies, according to the Committee report, was more than 2.5 billion dollars. The most infamous of these 11 companies is AmeriDebt.

✦ The Sad Case of Jolanta Troy

The Committee report contained the story of Jolanta Troy.

"An example of how the DebtWorks-Ballenger conglomerate treated its clients is illuminating. The Subcommittee interviewed Jolanta Troy, who was a 46-year-old mother of two children, ages eleven and sixteen, when she heard an AmeriDebt radio commercial. Ms. Troy had recently been divorced and began accumulating debt soon thereafter. Her job as a behavior specialist consultant working with mentally ill and behaviorally challenged children did not provide her with enough income to pay her $30,000 in credit card debt and support her children. Ms. Troy contacted AmeriDebt in 2001 and was informed by Vicky, an AmeriDebt 'counselor,' about the benefits of enrolling in a DMP. Ms. Troy told Vicky that she wanted to think about whether to sign up on a DMP, but soon thereafter received 3 to 4 additional calls from AmeriDebt, pressuring her to enroll.

Ms. Troy agreed to enroll and was told that her first payment would be $783. She was told to rush the payment by Western Union 'so that her bills would be paid on time.' Vicky told her that she could make a voluntary contribution at a later date when she was more financially stable. Ms. Troy mailed in her $783 payment, but continued to receive calls from creditors. She then called AmeriDebt to inquire about her account and was informed that AmeriDebt had kept her first payment and had sent nothing to her creditors. Ms. Troy requested a refund and was denied, even after complaining to the Better Business Bureau. Ms. Troy then believed her only option was to declare bankruptcy, which she did later that year. Needless to say, she received no counseling or education from AmeriDebt during any of their telephone conversations.

Ms. Troy's experience with AmeriDebt is, unfortunately, all too common. In addition, even if she had remained on AmeriDebt's DMP, the fee she was charged bears no relation to the value of the services that would have been provided to her by AmeriDebt.

The initial DMP start-up fee charged by AmeriDebt and the other ten CCAs in the DebtWorks-Ballenger conglomerate is based upon the consumer's aggregate debt, rather than the actual expense of initiating a DMP. Specifically, the consumer is generally asked to make a contribution equaling 3% of their aggregate debt. For example, if a consumer owes a total of $25,000, their initial fee would be $750 (3% of $25,000). In contrast, the start up fee at the average NFCC member agency for a consumer who owes $25,000 would be $23.09. Furthermore, as in the case of Ms. Troy, consumers are often left with the impression that this initial fee amount will be sent to their creditors, when in fact it is retained by the CCA. Aside from the initial start-up fee, the monthly DMP maintenance fees charged by Ballenger CCAs are based not upon AmeriDebt's actual costs or the value of the service to the consumer, but upon the number of credit cards on the plan—generally $7 per credit card with a minimum of $20 per month and a maximum of $70 per month."

Debt Can Be Profitable

The Senate Subcommittee found it particularly telling that AmeriDebt's employees were paid bonuses for enrolling customers in DMPs. The amount of the bonus depended on the number of consumers the employee enrolled in DMPs, along with how much money was actually collected in regard to the putting the DMP into effect. This was troubling to the Senate investigators who interpreted this as a clear conflict of interest because the AmeriDebt employees had a vested interest in enrolling consumers in DMPs rather than providing financial counseling to people for whom a DMP might not be advisable.

The Cambridge-Brighton Conglomerate

The Cambridge-Brighton conglomerate was another tangled web of related for-profit and non-profit companies that the Subcommittee found troubling.

The Subcommittee report detailed the story of one of its customers, Raymond Schuck.

"Mr. Schuck told the Subcommittee that, in the summer of 2001, he was $90,000 in debt distributed among nine credit cards. After hearing about Cambridge on the radio, he called them and spoke with a counselor. The counselor suggested a debt management plan, and promised a reduction in interest rates. After answering a list of questions about his various credit cards, the counselor told Mr. Schuck that his monthly payment would be $1,949 and that Cambridge would charge him 10% of his monthly payments for their services, or $194 a month. Mr. Schuck thought that $194 was high, but knew very little about the industry and assumed that, because Cambridge was a non-profit, he could trust them.

The counselor told Mr. Schuck to hurry and send the first monthly payment to Cambridge to get the program started. He immediately sent in a cashier's check. Although he had already sent in the check to Cambridge, Mr. Schuck started getting calls from some of his creditors asking why he had not made any payments. The creditors told him that they were unaware that he was on a DMP with Cambridge and stated that no payments had been received.

Mr. Schuck called Cambridge to find out what was going on. He found it very difficult to contact someone in customer service who could tell him about his account. When Mr. Schuck did speak with Cambridge, he was informed that the first payment he had sent was a fee for initiating his DMP. He was shocked by this information, and told the Subcommittee that had he known of that in advance, he would have searched for a different credit counseling agency. Mr. Schuck said he would never have agreed to give Cambridge almost $2,000 when that money could have gone to his creditors. Ultimately, Mr. Shuck declared bankruptcy. Mr. Schuck felt that if Cambridge had done a reasonable analysis of his financial circumstances, the proper recommendation would have been to seek legal assistance and declare bankruptcy."

Fees, Fie, Foe, Fum

According to the Subcommittee investigation, the fees of Cambridge-Brighton were the most expensive of any of the credit counseling agencies that the Subcommittee looked into. Again, the Subcommittee concluded that the fees had no relationship whatsoever to either the cost of setting up or maintaining a debt management plan. The initial start-up fee, called a "Payment Design Fee," was generally set at an amount equal to the client's monthly payment amount. The Subcommittee noted that "The vast majority of monthly payments are several hundred dollars and many are in excess of $1,000 or even close to $2,000. As such, the Cambridge-Brighton CCAs routinely charge a consumer $500 or $1,000 for merely setting up a DMP. Like AmeriDebt and other Ballenger CCAs, the Cambridge-Brighton CCAs retain this fee instead of sending it to creditors. Also like AmeriDebt, the Cambridge-Brighton CCAs often fail to adequately disclose that fact. Like many other consumers who dealt with Cambridge, Mr. Schuck was not informed that his 'Payment Design Fee' of $1,949 would not go to his creditors, but would in fact be kept by Cambridge."

But the fees did not end there. Cambridge-Brighton also tacked on a monthly "Program Service Fee" that was calculated as a percentage of the monthly DMP payment. This fee was set at ten percent of the monthly DMP payment. So a Cambridge-Brighton client paying, for example, a monthly payment amount of $900 through his or her DMP would be paying an additional $90 every month just as a service fee. If, in this example, the DMP had a duration of three years, the client would end up paying an extra $3,240 in monthly service fees alone. It is noteworthy to contrast this fee with the average NFCC member agency's monthly maintenance fee for a DMP that in 2002 was $14. In the previous example of a three-year DMP with monthly payments of $900, the difference in maintenance fees between Cambridge-Brighton CCAs and a NFCC member agency would be $2,736, a considerable amount of money, particularly if you are counting your pennies and trying to pay your debts.

Credit Counseling

As for counseling, you had better look elsewhere because you will not get it at Cambridge-Brighton CCAs. Similar to the situation at AmeriDebt, the so-called credit counselors of Cambridge-Brighton CCAs were paid bonuses based upon the amount of start-up fees for DMPs they produced each month. Raymond Shuck received a grand total of 20 minutes of counseling before he was advised to send in his first check for $1,949 to get his DMP rolling.

Legal Problems for AmeriDebt

The legal actions brought against AmeriDebt by the Federal Trade Commission, as well as the attorneys general for the states of Missouri, Maryland, Illinois, Minnesota, and Texas, exemplify the concerns about misrepresentations made by credit counseling agencies. The charges allege that AmeriDebt engaged in deceptive practices by misrepresenting their fees, their operation as a non-profit organization, and their role in instructing consumers about how to handle their finances.

According to the various law enforcement officials from the FTC and the states bringing actions against the company, AmeriDebt publicly claimed that it was a non-profit organization whose primary purpose was to help consumers deal with their personal financial problems. However, according to these law enforcement officials, the truth is that AmeriDebt did not operate for this charitable purpose, but rather operated to generate profits for its affiliated companies. The so-called "credit counselors" or "debt professionals," according to Missouri Attorney General Jay Nixon, were more accurately described as salespeople who were partially compensated through commissions on the fee-generating debt repayment programs they sold. According to Attorney General Nixon, these salespeople were not trained as credit counselors and provided no real financial education to their customers. And the costs did not end there. AmeriDebt, it was alleged, also charged their customers fees of as much as seventy dollars per month for the entire duration of the debt repayment plan, which often stretched to as long as five years.

The complaints against AmeriDebt also alleged that rather than teach customers about money and debt management, the company had the same solution for all customers: a "debt management plan" that required its customers to make a regular monthly payment to the company that then paid all the customer's creditors. Beyond the obvious problems of having the same solution to every individual's problems, regardless of their circumstances, a major flaw with this so-called solution is that, according to the FTC and state attorneys general complaints, the first monthly payment made by the customer went to AmeriDebt as a fee. Typically, this payment amounted to three percent of the consumer's total debt. So rather than having their debts start to be paid off, AmeriDebt's customers found themselves going deeper into debt. This practice by AmeriDebt was alleged to be even more deceptive because AmeriDebt claimed in its advertising that it did not charge any up-front fees. The AmeriDebt contract refers to this fee as "voluntary," but the FTC and the states' attorneys general argued that the fee was anything but voluntary. According to Howard Beales, the director of the FTC's Bureau of Consumer Protection, "We will not allow consumers to be duped into 'contributing' hundreds of dollars to these so-called 'non-profits.' There was nothing voluntary and nothing charitable about these payments. Consumers' money didn't go to creditors, it just ended up lining the pockets of the defendants."

More Horror Stories

In 2003 the Federal Trade Commission and National Credit Repair settled an FTC civil complaint against National Credit Repair and others that alleged that National Credit Repair and five other related defendants engaged in false and deceptive claims regarding their credit repair services. As a condition of the settlement, National Credit Repair, one of the country's largest credit repair organizations, agreed to pay 1.15 million dollars in consumer redress. It should be noted that in agreeing to the settlement, National Credit Repair did not admit that it violated the law; however, it did promise never to do it again and did agree to pay 1.15 million dollars for its actions that it says did not violate the law.

National Credit Repair has been involved with credit repair services since 1996, and between that year and 2003 had sold its credit repair services to more than 183,000 people. The actions that got them in trouble with the FTC consisted of claiming that they could remove derogatory information from their customers' credit reports, even if that information was both timely and accurate. The way they proposed to achieve this end, which people should have recognized as unrealistic, was through what they called a "one of a kind" computer disc that the company claimed could locate and identify mistakes in the process used by the credit reporting agencies to enter negative items such as foreclosures, bankruptcies, and late payments on consumers' credit reports. Not surprisingly, the FTC found those representations to be both false and deceptive. It also should be noted that as a part of the settlement, National Credit Repair agreed not to make these claims for their discs or software in the future. In truth, there was no such disc or software program. What National Credit Repair was actually selling was just a program through which they sent letters to the credit reporting agencies disputing the accuracy of every negative bit of information contained within the consumer's credit report. These are the same dispute letters that anyone can send on their own and are not capable of removing accurate, verifiable information that is still timely.

There Ought to Be a Law

The rules that govern the credit counseling industry are a hodge-podge of state and federal statutes, tax laws, professional association standards, and creditor guidelines. By the way, a hodge-podge is described in the dictionary as a medley or an indiscriminate mixture. I prefer the old English synonym however of "gallimaufry." Try that one on for size.

The two major trade associations for the credit counseling industry are the NFCC and the Association of Independent Consumer Credit Counseling Agencies (AICCCA), both of which have excellent standards to which their members must adhere. The only problem is that adherence to these association standards is limited to only those companies who join these two associations. Being a member of either organization is entirely voluntary, and the companies that are the biggest offenders in the credit counseling industry merely choose not to align with either entity. In addition, neither organization is in a position to enforce its standards. Those companies already inclined to act in an ethical manner for the benefit of needy consumers will do so, regardless of whether there are rules or not. The companies inclined to ignore the needs of consumers by placing their own profits before the needs of their customers are free to ignore the association-established rules and standards.

That being said, it is still relatively important to note that an NFCC member credit counseling agency agrees to

1. Set aside a reasonable amount of money for consumer educational programs having to do with money management, budgeting, and the intelligent use of credit.

2. Make sure that their credit counselors perform comprehensive money management counseling interviews with clients.

3. Keep their fees as low as possible. It is also important to note that according to the NFCC rules, no one may be refused the services of a member credit counseling agency due to his or her inability to pay the usual fees.

The AICCCA specifically sets a maximum initial fee of $75 for establishing a DMP and limits the maximum amount of the fee for managing a DMP to $50 per month.

Creditor Standards

Because of the reliance by many credit counseling agencies on the fair share payments that they receive from the credit card companies and other creditors, those creditors have an inordinate amount of influence upon the operation of the credit counseling industry. As the expenses of the credit card issuers have increased in recent years, the fair share payment percentages have gone down. According to an April 2003 report of the Consumer Federation of America and the National Consumer Law Center, the rates for fair share payments for the major credit card issuers are now between zero and ten percent. The NFCC reported in 2002 that the average fair share payment from creditors that it received was around eight percent. In addition, some creditors have gone to performance-based fair share plans by which the amount of money that the credit counseling agency receives as a fair share payment is related to the success rates of the DMPs from that particular credit counseling agency.

In the course of its investigation, the Senate Permanent Subcommittee looked into the creditor standards of Bank One, MBNA America, and Citigroup, three large credit card issuers, and found that Bank One and MBNA have moved to minimum standards and performance based conditions for fair share payments. In both instances, the minimum standards include accreditation of the agency as well as other helpful, consumer-friendly standards. In addition, MBNA also limits the start up fees to $75 and the monthly fees to $50.

Citigroup has come up with its own unique model for fair share payments that uses a program through which Citigroup makes payments to credit counseling agencies according to its "perception of the agency's needs and the benefits they provide to the customer and the community."

Again, the problem is less with the standards of each of these three major creditors than with their ability and willingness to monitor and enforce their own policies.

How Do You Choose a Credit Counseling Agency?

1. Do some comparison shopping. Check out a few different agencies and do not give them any personal financial information about you before you have made up your mind.

2. Limit your choices to credit counseling agencies that are affiliated with either the NFCC or the AICCCA and which adhere to their standards.

3. Check out the particular company with the consumer protection division of your state attorney general's office and the Federal Trade Commission. Make sure there are not a lot of complaints lodged against them.

4. Go to their offices. Do not pick a company entirely through the Internet or over the phone.

5. Make sure that they offer serious counseling and not just debt management plans. See what is the range of services they provide.

6. Check out the costs. Make sure you know what all the fees are. If you are in particularly dire financial straits, see if they will waive their fees.

7. Confirm that they do not share any of your personal information without your approval. Such information sharing increases the danger of identity theft.

8. Make sure that the agency's employees are not on commission for signing you up for a debt management plan.

Will Working with a Credit Counseling Service Hurt Your Credit?

Well, it certainly won't hurt it as much as having a bankruptcy on your record for ten years. Your FICO score does not consider the fact that you are dealing with a credit counseling service in determining your credit score. It neither helps you nor hurts you. It does not take the proverbial rocket scientist to guess, however, that failing to pay your bills or being late with your payments will hurt your credit score. It is important to note that regardless of what your credit score is, the ultimate decision as to whether or not to grant you future credit will be made by the bank, credit card company, or whatever other company with which you may be dealing at the time. They all have their own criteria. Some consider your working with a credit counseling service, particularly if you adhere to the program, as a positive indication that you are taking affirmative steps to control your debt problems and that you are acting responsibly.

Do-It-Yourself Credit Repair

Sometimes there is nothing wrong with your credit. There is just something wrong with your credit report. Many credit reports contain inaccurate information that can have a harmful effect on future credit applications by you. The first step toward fixing these commonly occurring errors is to identify them. Sometimes these errors may be the result of an identity thief accessing your accounts or establishing new accounts in your name. Other times these errors are just mistakes that can happen anywhere in the credit process, such as when someone with a name similar to yours has their negative credit information reported on your credit report. In any event, it is important to regularly monitor your credit report at least annually. In this way, you can locate discrepancies before they become a problem, such as when you are in the process of applying for a mortgage.

What Do You Look For?

When you get your credit report, go through it carefully and note any mistakes or misinformation. The items on a credit report that are considered the most serious and have the greatest effect on your credit score are in descending order:

1. Bankruptcies

2. Foreclosures

3. Repossessions of automobiles or other goods

4. Defaults on loans

5. Court judgments

6. Collection actions

7. Past due payments

8. Late payments

9. Credit rejections

10. Credit inquiries

After you have identified a problem in your credit report, if it is found to be outdated (over seven years old for most debts), you have a right under federal

---

law to require the credit reporting agency reporting this misinformation to investigate the matter and remove it from your report , a mistake, or even if it merely can no longer be verified.

A Small But Significant Piece of Advice

Because each of the three major credit reporting agencies operate independently of each other, it is important to check all three versions of your credit report for inaccuracies.

Next Step

After you have identified the problem, notify the credit-reporting agency that you are disputing the accuracy of something that appears on your credit report. A form letter for notifying them is included in Chapter 15, "Form Letters." Request that they investigate the matter. It is important to be as specific as possible in requesting a correction of your credit report. Include copies of any documentation you may have to support your position, but do not send them original documents. If you have been a victim of identity theft, make sure you inform the credit reporting agency of this fact. Even if you have not been the victim of identity theft, but the information contained in your credit report is inaccurate, incomplete or stale, you may be able to get the credit reporting agency to correct your credit report following an investigation.

Words to the Wise

Even if you are not a Boy Scout, it is a good idea to always be prepared. When disputing information on your credit report, this means that you should always send your written communications to the credit-reporting agencies by certified mail. That way, if necessary later, you will be able to prove not only that the credit reporting agency received your letter, but also the date that they received it. This is particularly important because the law generally requires the credit reporting agency to complete its investigation within forty-five days of receiving your request.

Following an investigation, if the credit-reporting agency agrees that a mistake was made on your credit report, you may request that a copy of your credit report reflecting the corrections be sent to anyone who had received a copy of your credit report that contained the inaccurate information.

Be a Pack Rat

Believe it or not, after all of your hard work in getting improper information deleted from your credit report, you still may find that information reappear on your credit report. Therefore, it is both important to continually monitor your credit report and to keep any correspondence you may have from the credit reporting agency that indicated that the material was being deleted from your file earlier. Armed with this documentation, correcting the problem a second time should be much easier.

If, following a credit reporting agency's investigation of your complaint, they still insist that the information is accurate, you may wish to directly contact the creditor that is the source of the negative information to straighten out the matter. If you are able to do so, you should go back to the credit reporting agency armed with a written letter from the creditor that the harmful information contained in your credit report is indeed inaccurate to help speed up the process of correcting your report.

If, at this point, the credit reporting agency still insists that the information contained in your credit report is correct, the law entitles you to have your own written explanation of the matter included in your credit report. Do not be long winded. The law limits your explanation to one hundred words. Whether you are reviewing your credit report with an eye toward enhancing your credit score or to deal with damaged credit, the process and the law is the same. Go to Chapter 11, "Credit Reports," for further hints on dealing with your credit report.

Do-It-Yourself Credit Counseling

One of the first things you should do is take a good, hard look at yourself and determine what got you into credit or debt problems in the first place. You may have done absolutely nothing wrong except to have had the misfortune to get sick. Catastrophic medical care costs constitute one of the largest causes of many people's debt problems. Or maybe you lost your job or you got divorced. Or maybe, just maybe, you are one of those really unlucky people who became so distressed about your divorce that you got sick and lost your job in which case you just might have the right to sing the blues. However, perhaps you just have been overspending. It surely is easy enough to do. Stores encourage you to buy things. Television encourages you to buy things. Credit card companies encourage you to buy things. Even politicians encourage you to buy things as your patriotic duty to help the economy. But that being said, it is time for a little personal responsibility, and the plain, hard fact is that many of use just live and spend beyond our means. Deficit spending may work for the federal government, but it does not work for you and me. We cannot print money, or if we do, we go to jail, directly to jail and we don't pass go and we don't collect $200.

So now we have recognized that, as Tom Hanks calmly said in the movie *Apollo 13*, "Houston, we have a problem." What do you do next? The next logical step is to set up a budget. List all your regular fixed monthly expenses, such as your rent or mortgage, insurance premiums, and your car payment, if any. Then add to that list designated amounts for food, clothing, entertainment, and all the incidentals that make up the things on which you spend your money. For some helpful information and forms to help you budget, just Google "personal budgets" and you will find plenty of helpful information.

When you have figured out your budget, you should be able to see how much money you have available to pay off your creditors. Now it is time for you to contact them and make arrangements to pay them off over time. You might consider negotiating for lump sum reduced payments to your creditors or extending the time and reducing the amounts of your monthly payments; but whatever plan you work out, make sure it is one to which you can adhere.

Endnotes

1. United States Senate Permanent Subcommittee on Investigations Report, "Profiteering in a Non-Profit Industry (Abusive Practices in Credit Counseling" page 6, 2004)

13

CONGRESS DEALS WITH CREDIT REPORTS AND IDENTITY THEFT: THE FAIR AND ACCURATE CREDIT TRANSACTIONS ACT

Those who do not learn from history are doomed to repeat it."

I used to think about that George Santayana quote a lot, particularly while taking history courses. However, it also applies to Congress when they revisit legislation in order to improve it.

The Fair and Accurate Credit Transactions Act (FACT) was signed into law on December 4, 2003, by President George W. Bush, although many parts of the new law will be phased in over the next few years and a number of details of the new law were left to be worked out over the months and years following the signing of the law. The name of this law reflects present concerns of many Americans about the fairness and accuracy of their credit reports as well as concerns regarding privacy and identity theft.

The law was an amendment of the Fair Credit Reporting Act that was originally passed in 1970. At that time, the focus of the law was on providing consumers better access to the information contained in their credit reports. The Fair Credit Reporting Act was amended in 1996 primarily to deal with concerns about the accuracy of information found in credit reports and in recognition of consumer rights pertaining to credit reports, as well as in response to concerns about the accuracy of the information contained within those reports. The 1996 amendment of the law provided a number of new consumer rights. However, in return for those rights now guaranteed by federal law, the rights of the individual states to generally enact stronger consumer protection laws in this area of the law were preempted temporarily until January 1, 2004. It was the looming deadline of the federal preemption of state action regarding many credit and privacy related issues that made almost certain that financial industry lobbyists would press for legislation to be passed to extend those preemptions before the January 1, 2004 deadline. Fortunately for consumers, the fact that the financial industry was so anxious to have a law passed in a timely fashion also made financial institution lobbyists a bit more willing to compromise on some matters to the benefit of consumers; although, make no mistake about it, this law is one written to protect the financial industry in this country. But one would have to be the ultimate negativist not to recognize that there are significant new benefits to consumers contained within FACT to improve accuracy of credit reports and help in the fight against identity theft.

Major Provisions of FACT

"Just the facts ma'am," the line attributed to Jack Webb as Sgt. Joe Friday in the Classic 1951–1957 television crime show *Dragnet* was never actually spoken by Jack Webb on the show. The line is just a cultural myth. However the Fair and Accurate Credit Transactions Act (FACT) is not a myth. It is the law and it is filled with important provisions. It deals with a number of different facets of credit reporting. One of its primary goals is to enhance the accuracy of the entire credit reporting system. It also has a number of provisions that deal with credit reporting and identity theft. Finally, it provides for a number of continuing studies of various areas, including credit scoring, technological advances in identity verification, and financial literacy in order to set the stage for future legislation. What follows are summaries of some of the important provisions of FACT.

Free Credit Reports
One of the major benefits of FACT is the provision that requires credit-reporting agencies to provide consumers, upon request, a free copy of their

credit report annually within 15 days of the date of the request. Credit reporting agencies formerly charged for this service, except in Colorado, Georgia, Maine, Maryland, Massachusetts, New Jersey, and Vermont, where state law already provided for an annual free report. You may expect to receive a host of solicitations for other services of the credit-reporting agencies with your free credit report as they take advantage of this law as a marketing opportunity.

Due to a concern about the flooding of the credit reporting agencies with requests for free credit reports, the requirement of free credit reports will be phased in through September 1, 2005. Residents of Alaska, Arizona, California, Colorado, Hawaii, Idaho, Montana, Nevada, New Mexico, Oregon, Utah, Washington, and Wyoming could request a free report as of December 1, 2004. Residents of Illinois, Indiana, Iowa, Kansas, Michigan, Minnesota, Missouri, Nebraska, North Dakota, Ohio, South Dakota, and Wisconsin are eligible for free credit reports as of March 1, 2005. Residents of Alabama, Arkansas, Florida, Georgia, Kentucky, Louisiana, Mississippi, Oklahoma, South Carolina, Tennessee, and Texas may obtain free credit reports beginning June 1, 2005. And residents of Connecticut, Delaware, Maine, Maryland, Massachusetts, New Hampshire, New Jersey, New York, North Carolina, Pennsylvania, Rhode Island, Vermont, Virginia, and West Virginia become eligible for free credit reports as of September 1, 2005.

Reinvestigations Following Review of Free Credit Report

FACT gives the credit reporting agencies 45 days in which to conduct a reinvestigation of any discrepancies discovered by consumers after reviewing their free annual credit reports.

Summary of Rights

Having rights in regard to your credit is only of use to you if you are aware of your rights in this complicated area of consumer rights. FACT requires the FTC to make available a summary of the rights of consumers under the law. This summary of rights will be given to consumers who are denied credit or offered credit at less favorable terms as a result of information contained in their credit reports. The FTC is also required to generally promote the availability of this summary of rights and provide it on the FTC website. The summary of rights must include information describing when a consumer may obtain a free copy of his or her credit report, the right to dispute information in the consumer's credit report, and the right to obtain his or her credit score. The summary of rights must also include toll free telephone numbers for all federal agencies involved with FACT and a notice to consumers that they may have additional rights under their own state's laws.

Fraud Alerts

In the past, people who were the victims of identity theft were routinely told to contact the three major credit-reporting agencies, Equifax, Experian, and TransUnion, to have a fraud alert placed on their credit report at each of the three credit reporting agencies. A single telephone call to any of the big three would permit you to put a fraud alert on your account. That was the good news. A fraud alert is a notice placed prominently on your credit report that informs creditors and those considering granting you credit that you have been, or are in imminent danger of becoming, a victim of identity theft due to the privacy of your personal financial information being compromised. A fraud alert usually listed your telephone number, and in an effort to avoid further identity theft damages, a request that you be called before granting further credit applied for in your name. But the key word in that last sentence was "request." The bad news was that until FACT was passed, the use of fraud alerts was completely voluntary on the part of creditors. Until now, many businesses granting credit would only look at a summary report or credit score report prepared by the credit-reporting agency. Because the fraud alert was only included on the full credit report, many businesses extending credit never saw the fraud alerts. In addition, many creditors just did not bother to even check for fraud alerts when granting credit, thereby rendering them useless.

Fortunately, the rules regarding fraud alerts have been both codified and strengthened by FACT. The new law recognizes the right of consumers to contact any of the three major credit-reporting agencies and have a fraud alert placed on their files at each of those credit-reporting agencies whenever the consumer has a good-faith suspicion that either he or she has been a victim of fraud or identity theft, or that he or she is about to become a likely victim of such a crime.

An initial fraud alert must include information that notifies anyone who is considering the consumer's credit report for business purposes that the consumer does not authorize the establishment of any new credit or extension of present credit without the specific permission of the consumer. The initial alert also has a place for the consumer to provide a telephone number to be used for identity verification when credit is sought in the consumer's name.

The initial fraud alert remains on the consumer's credit report for 90 days, however, an extended fraud alert can remain, at the consumer's request, on his or her credit report for up to seven years if the consumer provides an identity theft report to the credit reporting agency. The identity theft report can take the form of the Federal Trade Commission's Identity Theft Affidavit if that affidavit has been filed with a law enforcement agency. The FTC's Identity Theft Affidavit is reproduced in Chapter 15, "Form Letters." Whenever a credit score is calculated for a creditor or prospective creditor reviewing the file for credit granting purposes, the fraud alert must be included with the credit score. Unlike the situation before the passing of FACT, anyone or any business that uses credit reports and the credit scores calculated from the information contained therein now is required to honor the fraud alert.

A further benefit of placing an extended fraud alert on your credit report is that for the next five years you are automatically taken off of the pre-screened lists regularly provided by the credit-reporting agencies to credit card issuers and insurance companies sending out the offers that clutter our mailboxes and make us more susceptible to identity theft.

Anyone placing a fraud alert on his or her credit report also has the right to a free copy of his or her credit report within three business days of requesting a copy. Those people placing an extended fraud alert on their files are also eligible to receive two free copies of their credit report during the twelve month period following the filing of the extended fraud alert. The consumer is free to choose when he or she wants to receive these free reports.

Active duty military personnel have their own special provisions for fraud alerts. A person on active duty with the military, including someone who is in the reserves but serving at somewhere other than his or her usual station, may request an active duty alert that becomes a part of his or her credit report for the next 12 months. For the next 24 months, he or she will be automatically opted out of pre-screened offer lists.

Blocking of Information

Credit reporting agencies are required by FACT to block any negative information that appears on the consumer's credit report as a result of the consumer being the victim of identity theft. In order to qualify for blocking of such information, the consumer must provide the credit reporting agency with a copy of the identity theft report filed by him or her with a law enforcement agency, which again emphasizes how important it is to report all instances of identity theft to federal or state law enforcement officials. After the consumer has filed this report with the credit-reporting agency, it must promptly notify the company that provided the false information that the information provided by them may be the result of an identity theft, that an identity theft report has been filed, and an information block requested. After they have been so notified, the provider of information that has been blocked must institute procedures to prevent the erroneous blocked information from being resubmitted to the credit reporting agencies.

Business Records Disclosure

This new provision of FACT permits a victim of identity theft to directly contact businesses where an identity thief may have opened accounts or purchased goods or services in the identity theft victim's name, and upon presentation of a police report get copies of that business' records to help the consumer start the often long process of clearing his or her name.

Red Flag Guidelines for New Accounts and Change of Address Verification

FACT requires the FTC, federal banking agencies, and the National Credit Union Administration to identify specific patterns and indicators of identity theft and come up with guidelines for use by credit card issuers and others. One specific mandate of the law is that regulations be drafted to provide for the situation where a card issuer is contacted by someone requesting a change of address for an existing account or requesting an additional or replacement credit card in order to confirm that the person making the address change or requesting the new card is not an identity thief.

Credit Card Number Truncation

Credit card numbers imprinted on receipts are an important source of information for identity thieves who often obtain this information by rummaging through trash. FACT requires all receipts that are electronically printed to truncate the numbers of the credit card so that no more than the last five digits of the card number appear on any sales receipt. Although full compliance with this provision of the law is not required until the year 2007, many companies are already following this prudent practice.

Social Security Number Truncation

Under FACT, a consumer may request that the credit reporting agencies truncate his or her Social Security number where it appears on his or her credit report whenever a consumer's credit report is sent out. This is important in order to reduce the number of people having access to this sensitive information.

Banning of Collecting Debts Resulting from Identity Theft

When an identity theft victim has filed an identity theft report with both a law enforcement agency and with the credit-reporting agency, as well as notified the business where the identity theft debt originated, that particular business may not attempt to collect that debt from the identity theft victim. In addition, it may not sell that debt to anyone or place the debt with a collection agency.

Mortgage Lenders Are Now Required to Provide Credit Scores and Other Credit-related Information

Your credit score is a key element in not only determining whether or not you will be granted a mortgage loan by a bank or mortgage company, but also at what interest rate the loan will be offered to you. A difference of a quarter of a point or a half of a point on the interest rate that you are offered because of your credit score can have a substantial effect on the cost of your mortgage to you. The new law not only requires that your credit score be disclosed to you by the mortgage lender, but you must also be told about the key factors that may have brought your score down. This gives consumers the opportunity to discover mistakes in their credit report that, when corrected, can improve their score.

The federal government giveth and the federal government taketh away. Although this provision of the new law can be very helpful to consumers, the law also prohibits the individual states from enacting their own stronger laws pertaining to disclosures of credit scores when credit is being granted. Already existing laws in California and Colorado, however, were "grandfathered," and are allowed to continue in force.

Other Disclosure of Credit Scores

FACT also gives consumers the right to require the credit-reporting agencies to provide them with not only their current credit scores, but a notice that includes the range of possible credit scores under the credit scoring system used and an indication of as many as five key factors that may have adversely affected the credit score of the consumer. Consumers must also receive a notice disclosing the fact that the information and credit scoring model that may be used by the lender or credit card company with which they may be dealing may by different than the credit score model being disclosed to them. A "fair and reasonable" fee may be charged by the credit reporting bureaus for providing the credit score of the consumer.

Single Notice of Furnishing Negative Information

Any financial institution that provides negative information about a consumer to a credit-reporting agency must also notify the consumer that this is being done. However, the credit-reporting agency is only required to do this the first time that they provide such negative information to the credit-reporting agencies. This notice may be included with the regular monthly billing statement or a notice of default. It may not be included with the consumer disclosures required by the Truth in Lending laws. The fact that this notice is only required a single time again emphasizes the necessity of regularly reviewing your accounts in detail in order to protect your credit.

Risk-based Pricing Notice

Another new provision of FACT is the requirement that when a consumer is either denied credit or required to pay more for credit as a result of negative information contained in the consumer's credit report, the consumer must be sent an adverse action notice that will, in turn, trigger the consumer's rights to a free credit report. This notice may be provided in advance to the consumer at any time during the application process. The law specifically authorizes the FTC to make regulations to modify the timing of the providing of this notice. Prior to FACT, a consumer may not have been aware that he or she was paying a higher interest rate because of information contained in his or her credit report. Again, preemption of state regulation rears its ugly head and the states are prohibited from extending consumers' rights within the individual states beyond the level prescribed by FACT in regard to this notice.

Future Rules Regarding Accuracy and Integrity of Information

The FTC, along with other federal regulators, is required by FACT to establish further rules and regulations in the future to provide for greater accuracy and integrity of information in credit reports. The FTC is also directed by FACT to identify patterns and practices that reduce the accuracy and integrity of information contained in credit reports.

Higher Standards for Providers of Information to Credit-Reporting Agencies

Prior to the enactment of FACT, any provider of information to the credit-reporting agencies, such as a credit card company that might report the history of a particular account, was only required to meet what I call the "Sergeant Schultz" standard. Sergeant Schultz was the role played by the late actor John Banner in the 1960's situation comedy *Hogan's Heroes*. Sergeant Schultz was famous for his constant refrain of "I know nothing. Noooothing!" that was said in order to avoid any responsibility or personal involvement. Until the passage of FACT, the standard for providers of information to credit-reporting agencies was that they were not permitted to report information that they knew was inaccurate or consciously avoided knowing that the information was inaccurate. The new higher standard is that the furnisher may not report any information if the furnisher "knows or has reasonable cause to believe that the information is inaccurate."

The Right of Consumers to Dispute Inaccurate Information Directly with the Furnisher

Prior to FACT, if a consumer disputed the accuracy of information reported by a creditor or other provider of information to the credit reporting bureaus, he or she had to request an investigation regarding the accuracy of the information from the credit reporting agency that in turn, had to request an investigation as to the accuracy of the information by the provider of the information. Now the consumer has the right to go directly to the individual furnishers of information and request that they reinvestigate the disputed information reported to the credit reporting agencies. This right is subject to FTC regulations. It is important to note that credit repair organizations will not be authorized to make requests on behalf of individual consumers for reinvestigation of disputed items.

FTC Required to Report on Credit Report Complaints

FACT was envisioned as a work in progress, recognizing that in the world of credit and technology circumstances are constantly changing. For this reason, many of the details of FACT were left to be worked out by the FTC and other agencies. In addition, in order to identify problems and to set the stage for future modifications of the law, the FTC was ordered to prepare annual reports on the complaints made by consumers as to the functioning of the credit-reporting agencies.

Disclosures of Results of Reinvestigation

In order to improve the accuracy of consumer credit reports, FACT requires the credit-reporting agencies to notify the furnishers of information when changes are made to a consumer's credit report after a change on the report has been made following a reinvestigation requested by the consumer. When the furnisher of information is informed of the change in the credit report, the furnisher must have its own procedures in place to block out that incorrect information that may have resulted from identity theft in order to prevent such information from being resubmitted erroneously to the credit-reporting agency.

Notification of Address Discrepancy

As a way of reducing identity theft, FACT requires credit-reporting agencies to notify anyone requesting a credit report on a particular consumer when the consumer's address on the request is different from the address as shown on the credit report.

Future Studies of Ways to Improve FACT

Congress recognized that FACT was just the next step in the evolution of more accurate credit reporting and the battle against identity theft. The next steps in this process may be determined by the results of studies that the FTC is required to do in the nine years following the enactment of FACT into law. Some of the specific items that the FTC and others must consider and report on are as follows:

1. Whether requiring confirmation of more identifying information in the process of requesting credit reports would serve to increase the accuracies of the credit reports and reduces identity theft

2. Whether informing consumers when negative information is added to their credit reports will enhance the ability of consumers to both identify errors on their credit reports and remove fraudulent information contained on their credit report as a result of identity theft.

3. Whether consumers receiving copies of their credit reports immediately following an adverse action based on information contained on their credit reports will help reduce mistaken information and remove fraudulent identity theft information appearing in consumer credit reports.

4. How to encourage reporting of information that presently goes unreported to the credit-reporting agencies that could better determine a consumer's creditworthiness. Interestingly, some lenders do not report their customers' timely loan payment history to the credit-reporting agencies due to a concern that other lenders will see this information and seek to lure away these good customers. Yet the consumer is the one hurt by this practice because information that might help increase his or her credit score goes unreported.

5. Whether biometrics and other technological advances can be used to help combat identity theft.

New Opt Out Rules for Prescreened Credit Offers

The offers of "preapproved" credit cards with which many of us are flooded can be not only an annoyance but a source of identity theft if a criminal gets a hold of the offers that so many of us just routinely toss into the waste basket. FACT now requires that such prescreened offers must prominently contain a telephone number, the use of which will permit the consumer to opt out of receiving further offers. Under prior law, the duration of a telephone opt out was two years. This has been increased to five years. The FTC was also ordered to increase consumer awareness of the entire opting out process.

New Opt Out Rules for Marketing Solicitations

For the first time, the law now requires that consumers be given the opportunity to opt out of having their personal information shared for marketing purposes with the affiliates of a company with which they do business. A consumer opt out in this situation will last for five years. Under this new rule, for instance, a bank with which you presently have an account would have to ask you prior to sharing your information with a company with which it is affiliated that sells insurance. Unfortunately, this new rule is filled with exemptions that water down the effectiveness of the rule. Privacy advocate and Maryland Senator Paul Sarbanes commented on this part of FACT saying, "I would have liked to have gone further... in the affiliate sharing section to provide more protection for the financial privacy of consumers...."

Study of Information Sharing

Whether you characterize it as a bone thrown to consumers or a first step toward some meaningful reform of the laws that regulate information sharing, FACT requires the FTC and other federal agencies to study and report back to Congress on the issue of information sharing.

Credit Scoring Study

Congress continued its homework assignments to the FTC and other federal agencies by specifically requiring a study be done and a report to Congress be written on the effects of the use of credit scores and credit-based insurance scores on the availability, as well as the cost, of various financial services and products such as credit cards, mortgages, automobile loans, and insurance.

For example, many insurance companies use the information contained in your credit report and your credit score to determine whether you present a higher likelihood of bringing an insurance claim which, of course, affects the insurance company's decision as to whether to sell you an insurance policy and at what premium level. Using credit reports and credit scores to make insurance decisions is highly controversial, and critics of this practice argue it is not rationally based. Critics of the practice also say that it violates the Equal Credit Opportunity Act that prohibits credit discrimination on the basis of sex, race, marital status, religion, national origin, age, or receipt of public assistance.

Establishment of the Financial Literacy Education Commission

FACT mandated the establishment of the Financial Literacy Education Commission to be made up of representatives of a number of different federal agencies and overseen by the Secretary of the Treasury. The goal of the Commission will be to come up with a national strategy to effectively promote financial literacy and education.

Preemption of State Laws

When the original Fair Credit Reporting Act was enacted into law in 1970, the law provided for federal protection of consumers in the areas of credit and credit reporting, but permitted the individual states to enact their own laws that would enhance consumer rights in these areas of the law. When the Fair Credit Reporting Act was amended in 1996, Congress specified seven particular provisions of the FCRA regarding which the states would be preempted from enacting stronger consumer laws until January 1, 2004. It was this deadline that provided the impetus for the financial services industry to pressure Congress to enact FACT before the January 1, 2004 deadline. Otherwise, the financial services industry would have most likely been made subject to a host of stronger laws passed by the individual states to protect their citizens. Fortunately, the impending deadline also made the financial services industry a bit more willing to compromise in some areas because of the risk of not having legislation passed before 2004. The bad news is that FACT makes permanent the seven areas of federal preemption, thus limiting the states from enacting stronger consumer protection laws in those seven covered areas. FACT also significantly limited the ability of the states to strengthen provisions of FACT in areas that were new to FACT, such as the area of risk-based pricing notices.

Fortunately, when it came to the burgeoning area of identity theft legislation, FACT only limits the states' powers to pass laws to reduce identity theft where state laws would deal with matters that were specifically dealt with by FACT such as the truncation of credit card numbers on receipts. Where something affecting identity theft was not specifically covered within FACT, the states are still free to pass their own tougher laws. In the past, the states have taken the lead in protecting consumers from identity theft, so this part of FACT is good news. For instance, California and Texas both have laws still available to their citizens that permit consumers to freeze their credit reports and prevent any new credit from being granted without the consumer specifically unfreezing the account through the use of a personal identification number. Bad news, however, is that some laws that served to protect citizens of individual states have been invalidated by FACT.

14

STEVE'S RULES

Following these rules can help you protect yourself from identity theft. The rules also will tell you what to do if you do become a victim of identity theft. If you have debt problems, these rules will instruct you about the best ways to deal with credit counselors and the traps to avoid. These rules will also help you understand your credit report and your credit score, as well as tell you what you need to do to improve your all-important credit score. These are my rules, some of which I even follow.

Identity Theft Protection Rules

1. Never give personal information over the phone to anyone whom you have not called, and always be sure of to whom you are speaking.

2. Only carry the credit cards that you need to use in your wallet.

3. Never carry your Social Security card in your wallet. Where is that thing anyhow?

4. If you rent a car, destroy your copy of the rental agreement when you return the car.

5. Consider using a post office box rather than having mail delivered to your home.

6. If you don't use a post office box, use a locked mailbox at your home.

7. Do not bring your checkbook with you on vacation. Use traveler's checks or credit cards.

8. Keep copies of all your credit cards, front and back, as well as the telephone numbers for customer service.

9. Remove yourself from marketing lists for pre-approved credit cards. If you receive pre-approved credit card applications that you do not use, shred them.

10. Sign up for the National Do Not Call List.

11. Check your credit report at least once a year.

12. Check your Social Security Statement provided by the Social Security Administration annually.

13. When you get a new credit card, sign it immediately and call to activate it.

14. As much as possible, keep your credit card in sight when you make a purchase to prevent it from being "skimmed."

15. Try paying your bills online, but if you do mail checks, mail them directly from the post office.

16. Check your bank statements, telephone bills, credit card statements, and brokerage account statements monthly for unauthorized charges.

17. Do not download files from people you do not know.

18. Shred, shred, and shred all unnecessary financial records and pre-approved credit card offers.

19. Do not store your personal information on a laptop computer.

20. Use anti-virus software and update it regularly.

21. Set up a firewall on your computer.

22. Remove all personal information from your hard drive when you get rid of your computer.

23. Ask any business that has personal information about you as to their policy for the protection of that information.

24. Do not use your Social Security number as your driver's license number or on your health insurance card.

25. Do not store on your computer the passwords to frequently visited websites. Enter them every time you go to the website.

26. Avoid privately owned ATMs.

27. Lock your car and don't leave anything in it that you cannot risk losing.

Rules to Follow If You Are a Victim of Identity Theft

1. Notify the credit reporting agencies and have a fraud alert placed on your account with each agency.

2. Report the crime to the appropriate authorities where you live and where the fraud occurred. Use the FTC's ID Theft Affidavit.

3. Inform all your creditors that you have become a victim of identity theft.

4. Get new credit cards with new account numbers for all tainted accounts

5. Set up passwords for new accounts.

6. Change your PIN numbers (I know this is redundant because PIN is an acronym for Personal Identification Number, but it just sounds right).

7. When you close tainted accounts, make sure the accounts are reported to the credit reporting agencies as being closed at the customer's request due to identity theft.

8. Ask your creditors to notify each of the credit reporting agencies to remove erroneous and fraudulent information from your file.

9. If your checks are stolen, promptly notify your bank and close the account immediately..

10. Notify the check verification companies and request that they contact retailers that use their services to advise them not to accept checks from any checking accounts of yours that have been accessed by identity thieves.

11. Contact the creditors who have tainted accounts in your name and request that they initiate a fraud investigation. Get a copy of the completed investigation.

12. Send copies of those completed investigations to each of the credit reporting agencies and request that erroneous and fraudulent information be removed from your files.

13. If fraudulent charges do manage to appear on your credit report, notify the credit reporting agencies in writing and tell them that you dispute the information and request that such information be removed from your files.

Credit Counseling Rules

1. If you need credit counseling, only consider credit counseling agencies that are affiliated with either the National Foundation for Credit Counseling or the Association of Independent Consumer Credit Counseling Agencies.

2. Check out the particular company with the consumer protection division of your state attorney general's office and the Federal Trade Commission.

3. Go to their offices. Do not pick a company entirely through the Internet or by phone.

4. Make sure that they offer serious debt counseling and not just debt management plans.

5. Check out the costs. Make sure you know what all the fees are. If you are in particularly dire financial straits, ask if they will waive their fees.

6. Confirm that they do not share any of your personal information without your approval.

7. Make sure that the agency's employees are not on commission for enrolling you in a debt management plan.

8. Never participate in file segregation as a way of fixing your credit report.

Credit Report and Credit Scoring Rules

1. When settling an overdue bill, make a condition of the settlement that the creditor report the payment to the credit reporting bureaus as "paid satisfactorily."

2. Get a copy of your credit score and see how it may be improved.

3. Pay your bills on time.

4. Limit the number of credit cards you have to the minimum number you need.

5. When choosing a credit card, look online for the credit card that is most appropriate for you. If you pay off your balance in full each month, consider the cards with the lowest fees. If you carry a balance forward, check out the cards with the lowest interest rates.

6. Don't get credit cards that are issued by specific retailers.

7. When closing an account, make sure it is reported to the credit reporting bureaus as "closed at customer's request."

8. Consider, where appropriate, "aging" an account in accordance with the rules set by FFIEC.

9. Reduce your debt.

15

FORM LETTERS

W hat follows are various form letters that may be adapted to your own specific situation and used accordingly. It is prudent to send these letters by certified mail, return receipt requested, in order to have a record of exactly when your letter was both sent and received. Also included is a form developed by the FTC to guide and record your efforts to correct identity theft problems.

Letter to company with which you do business that has not been tainted by identity theft

Business name
Address
City, state zip code
Re: Joe Victim—Account #1234

Dear Sir or Madam,

I am the victim of identity theft and although the person using my identity without my authorization has not obtained access to my account with you, I am concerned about that possibility. Please contact me in order to arrange to have a password put on my account with you so that access to my account with you can only be accomplished through the use of my password.

I also request that a fraud alert be placed on my account, indicating that I have been the victim of identity theft and to emphasize that increased scrutiny should be used whenever you are contacted in regard to my account.

You may reach me by telephone at 123-456-7890 or at my e-mail address of info@joevictim.com.

Thank you for in advance for your assistance in this matter.

Sincerely,
Joe Victim

Letter to credit-reporting agency reporting identity theft

Credit reporting agency name
Address
City, state zip code
Re: Joe Victim—Social Security number 123-45-6789

Dear Sir or Madam,

Please be advised that I am the victim of identity theft. Without my authorization an account was opened with xyz in my name or my account with xyz was improperly accessed (whichever applies).

Please immediately place a fraud alert on my account in accordance with FACT.

You are also hereby notified that I am disputing the following items on my credit report: (describe disputed items)

Please forward to me a free copy of my credit report in accordance with the provisions of FACT. When I have reviewed the credit report, I may contact you if there are any other fraudulent or otherwise inaccurate entries on my report.

Thank you in advance for your assistance in this matter.

I may be reached at 123-456-7890 or by e-mail at info@joevictim.com

Sincerely,

Joe Victim

Letter to business involved with identity theft

Business name
Address
City, state zip code
Re: Joe Victim—Account number 1234

Dear Sir or Madam,

Please be advised that I am the victim of identity theft. Without my authorization or knowledge an account was opened with you in my name. Specifically (state the details of the identity theft such as a credit card was obtained in your name).

Please close this account immediately.

In accordance with my rights under FACT, I hereby request that you investigate this matter fully. Please also notify all of the credit reporting agencies and remove any negative information pertaining to this account from my credit report. Please also forward a letter to me, confirming that this has been done and acknowledging that charges made to this account are fraudulent.

Thank you in advance for your cooperation in this matter.
I may be reached at 123-456-7890 or by e-mail at info@joevictim.com

Sincerely,

Joe Victim

Fair Credit Billing Act letter

Business name
Billing inquires department
Address
City, state zip code
Re: Joe Victim—Account number 12234

Dear Sir or Madam,

Please be advised that I am hereby disputing the billing error in the amount of $_____ on my account. The amount is inaccurate because (give reason). I request that this error be corrected immediately and that any corresponding finance and/or other charges relating to this disputed amount be properly credited. Please also forward to me a revised and corrected statement of my account reflecting the correction of this error.

I am enclosing copies of (describe copies of documents enclosed to support your claim) in support of my claim.

I may be reached by telephone at 123-456-7890 or by e-mail at info@joevictim.com

Thank you in advance for your cooperation.

Sincerely,

Joe Victim

Letter of agreement to settle debt

Business name
Address
City, state zip code
Re: Joe Victim—Account number 12345

Dear Sir or Madam,

I hereby propose that in return for the payment on or before (proposed date) of $(amount of settlement offer) that any and all debts I may have to you be discharged and that you accept this payment as payment in full of any and all debts I may have to you. As a further condition of this settlement proposal, you hereby agree to notify all credit reporting agencies to which you report that the account is "paid as agreed" and that you will inform all of the credit reporting agencies to delete any references on any credit reports that indicate that the account is or ever was late. This agreement shall be binding upon the parties and their successors and assigns.

I am enclosing two copies of this letter. If you accept this settlement proposal, please sign where indicated and return a signed copy of this contract to me. This offer shall remain open until (latest date for acceptance of settlement offer).

Sincerely,

Joe Victim

I hereby agree to the terms of the above agreement.
Name of Business
Signature _____
Date

Letter requesting removal of credit inquiry from credit report

Name of business
Address
City, state zip code
Re: Joe Victim—Social Security number 012-34-5678—unauthorized credit inquiry

Dear Sir or Madam,

Upon reviewing my credit report prepared by (name of credit reporting agency), I found a credit inquiry by you indicated on my credit report that was not authorized by me. As I believe you understand, requesting my credit report and correspondingly having an inquiry noted on my report without my authorization is improper. Such an inquiry can also have a deleterious effect on my credit score. I therefore request that you promptly notify (name of credit reporting agency) and have the credit inquiry removed. Please also forward to me confirmation that this has been done.

Thank you in advance for your cooperation.
You may contact me by telephone at 122-456-7890 or by e-mail at info@joevictim.com

Sincerely,

Joe Victim

Letter disputing information contained on credit report

Complaint Department
Equifax
P.O. Box 740241
Atlanta, GA 30374

Or

TransUnion
P.O. Box 1000
Chester, PA. 19022

Or

Experian
P.O. Box 2104
Allen, TX 75013

Re: Joe Victim—Social Security number 123-45-6789

Dear Sir or Madam,

I hereby dispute the following indicated information improperly contained in my credit report. I have highlighted the disputed items on a copy of my credit report that is included with this letter.

Specifically, these items are improper because (state each disputed item and the reasons why the information is erroneous, inaccurate, incomplete or dated).

I am enclosing the following copies of documentation in support of my assertion: (list the specific documents enclosed; always send copies of documents, never originals).

In accordance with my rights under FACT, I request that you investigate this matter promptly and correct my credit report accordingly.

Thank you in advance for your cooperation.

You may reach me by telephone at 123-456-7890 or at my e-mail address of info@joevictim.com

Sincerely,

Joe Victim

Follow-up letter to credit-reporting agency

Equifax
P.O. Box 740241
Atlanta, GA 30374

Or

TransUnion
P.O. Box 1000
Chester, PA. 19022

Or

Experian
P.O. Box 2104
Allen, TX 75013

Re: Joe Victim—Social Security number 123-45-6789
      Dispute letter of (date of original letter)
Dear Sir or Madam,

On (date of original dispute letter) I sent you a letter notifying you of improper information appearing in my credit report in violation of FACT. This letter was sent to you by certified mail, return receipt requested and was received by you on (date of receipt). I am enclosing a copy of my letter and a copy of the return receipt indicating receipt of said letter.
Your failure to respond to my demand for correction of my credit report within thirty days is a violation of FACT. If I do not receive an appropriate response to my original demand letter within ten days of the date of this letter, I may, without further notice, report your failure to abide by FACT to the Federal Trade Commission or take other appropriate action.
You may reach me by mail or by telephone at 123-456-7890 or by e-mail at info@joevictim.com.

Sincerely,
Joe Victim

Opt out letter

Name of company
Company address
City, state zip code

Re: Opt out instructions for Account # _____

Dear Sir or Madam,

Please be advised that, in accordance with the Financial Services Modernization Act (Gramm-Leach-Bliley Act) you are hereby notified that you do not have my permission to share my personal information with non-affiliated third-party companies or individuals.

Please be advised that I am further notifying you, in accordance with FACT, that you do not have my permission to share either my personal information or information about my creditworthiness with any affiliated company of yours.

Please send me a written confirmation that you are honoring my personal privacy request.

I may be reached by telephone at 123-456-7890 or by e-mail at info@joevictim.com.

Thank you in advance for your cooperation.

Sincerely,

Joe Victim

Letter transferring a balance on a credit card

Customer Service Department
Credit Card Company name
Address
City, State and zip code

Re: Joe Victim
Transfer of balance of account #_____ and closing of
account

Dear Sir,
You are hereby notified to transfer the outstanding balance on my
(name of credit card) account number _____ to my new
account that is identified as follows: (Name of credit card such as Visa
or MasterCard), Account number _____, issued by (name of
new credit card issuer) whose address is
_____.

Upon completion of the transfer of my outstanding balance to my new
credit card, please close your account with me and notify me in writing
by mail that this action has been completed.

Please also notify the credit reporting agencies to which you report
that my account with you was closed at my request and that the
account was in good standing at the time that it was closed.

Thank you in advance for your assistance in this matter.
You may reach me by telephone at 123-456-7890 or by e-mail at
info@joevictim.com.

Sincerely,

Joe Victim

Letter to bank to close account following identity theft

Name of bank
Address
City, state zip code

Re: Joe Victim—Account number _____

Dear Sir or Madam,

I am writing to confirm my request made by telephone on (date of request to close account) in which I requested that my checking account be closed and no further access to said account be permitted except by me in person upon the presentation of conclusive personal identification. I have made this request because I have reason to believe that I am a victim of identity theft or am in great danger of becoming so.

Thank you in advance for your cooperation.

I may be contacted by telephone at 123-456-6789 or by e-mail at info@joevictim.com.

Sincerely,

Joe Victim

Letter to check-verification company

Name of check-verification company
Address
City, state and zip code

Re: Joe Victim
    Checking Account number _____

Dear Sir or Madam,
I am the victim of identity theft. Therefore, I am hereby requesting that
you not accept any checks from the above-designated account. I also
request that you notify any retailers who may use your services not to
accept any checks on my behalf with this account number.

Thank you in advance for your assistance.

You may contact me by telephone at 123-456-7890 or by e-mail at
info@joevictim.com.

Sincerely,

Joe Victim

Letter notifying bank of theft of ATM card

Name of bank
Address
City, state and zip code

Re: Joe Victim
   Account Number _____

Dear Sir or Madam,
I am writing to confirm my telephone conversation with (name of
bank employee to whom you spoke when you first reported the loss
of your ATM card) of (date of telephone conversation) in which I
reported that my ATM card has been lost or stolen. As I indicated by
telephone, please cancel the ATM card. I will personally come to the
bank to obtain a replacement ATM card.

I may be reached by telephone at 123-456-7890 or by e-mail at
info@joevictim.com.

Sincerely,

Joe Victim

Letter requesting an extended fraud alert

Fraud Alert
Equifax
P.O. Box 740241
Atlanta, GA 30374

Or

Fraud Alert
TransUnion
P.O. Box 1000
Chester, PA 19022

Or

Fraud Alert
Experian
P.O. Box 2104
Allen, TX 75013

Re: Joe Victim—Social Security number 123-45-6789

Dear Sir or Madam,

Please be advised that I am the victim of identity theft. In accordance
with FACT, I hereby request that an extended fraud alert be placed on
my credit report. In support of this request, as required by law, I am
enclosing an identity theft report. Also in accordance with the provisions of FACT, I hereby request that I be sent, at no charge, a copy of
my credit report.

Thank you in advance for your assistance in this matter.
I may be reached by telephone at 123-456-7890 or by e-mail at
info@joevictim.com.

Sincerely,

Joe Victim

Letter requesting blocking of information

Equifax
P.O. Box 740241
Atlanta, GA 30374

Or

TransUnion
P.O. Box 1000
Chester, PA 19022

Or

Experian
P.O. Box 2104
Allen, TX 75013

Re: Joe Victim—Social Security number 123-45-5678

Dear Sir or Madam,
Please be advised that I am the victim of identity theft, a result of
which is the reporting of negative information on my credit report. In
accordance with the provisions of FACT, I hereby request that such
negative information be blocked from my report. The specific information that I am requesting be blocked is as follows: (list negative information to be blocked from your credit report). As required by FACT
and in support of my request, I am including a copy of my identity
theft report filed with a law enforcement agency.

I also hereby request, in accordance with the provisions of FACT, that
you promptly notify the company or companies providing the false
and negative information that the information provided by them is the
result of an identity theft, that an identity theft report has been filed
and an information block requested.

Thank you in advance for your assistance in this matter.

I may be reached by telephone at 123-456-7890 or by e-mail at
info@joevictim.com

Sincerely,

Joe Victim

Letter to credit-reporting agencies requesting truncation of Social Security number

Equifax
P.O. Box 740241
Atlanta, GA 30374

Or

TransUnion
P.O. Box 1000
Chester, PA 19022

Or

Experian
P.O. Box 2104
Allen, TX 75013

Re: Joe Victim—Social Security number 123-45-6789

Dear Sir or Madam,

In accordance with the provisions of FACT I hereby request that my Social Security number be truncated wherever it appears on my credit report whenever my consumer credit report is sent out.

Thank you in advance for your assistance in this matter.

I may be reached by telephone at 123-456-7890 or by e-mail at info@joevictim.com

Sincerely,

Joe Victim

Letter requesting re-aging of credit card account

Customer Service Department
Credit Card Company name
Address
City, State and zip code

Re: Joe Victim
    Account number _____

Dear Sir or Madam,

In accordance with the rules of the Federal Financial Institutions
Examination Council, I hereby request that my account be re-aged and
reclassified as up-to-date in payments. I also request that you report
this new classification of my account to each of the three major credit-
reporting agencies. My recent account activity demonstrates my
renewed willingness and ability to repay my debt to you. As required
by the FFIEC, in order to qualify for re-aging of my account, it is at
least nine months old and I have made at least three consecutive
monthly payments or a payment equal to that amount. Please advise
me if you have additional standards for the re-aging of accounts.

Thank you in advance for your assistance in this matter.
You may reach me by telephone at 123-456-7890 or by e-mail at
info@joevictim.com

Sincerely,

Joe Victim

Letter canceling a credit card

Customer Service Department
Credit Card Company name
Address
City, State and zip code

Re: Joe Victim
    Cancellation of account number _____

Dear Sir or Madam,

I am writing to follow-up on my telephone conversation with (insert name of person with whom you spoke) with whom I spoke by telephone on (insert date) at time I cancelled my credit card that is designated as account number (insert account number). Please confirm in writing that the cancellation of the credit card has been completed and that the canceling of the card, as I requested, has been reported to the three major credit-reporting agencies as "closed at customer's request."

Thank you for your assistance in this matter.

You may reach me by telephone at 123-456-7890 or by e-mail at info@joevictim.com.

Sincerely,

Joe Victim

Second letter regarding canceling of credit card

Customer Service Department
Credit Card Company name
Address
City, State and zip code

Re: Joe Victim
    Cancellation of account number _____

Dear Sir or Madam,

I am writing to follow up on my letter to you of (insert date), a copy of which is enclosed herewith, in which I confirmed the canceling of my credit card and the closing of my account. At that time I also confirmed my previous request made by telephone on (insert date) that the closing of my account be reported to the three major credit-reporting agencies as being "closed at customer's request." I have recently reviewed my credit report and my account with you is not designated in that fashion. Please correct this immediately.

Thank you in advance for your assistance in this matter.

You may reach me by telephone at 123-456-7890 or by e-mail at info@joevictim.com

Sincerely,

Joe Victim

Record of Identity Theft Communications

Use these tables to record all communications taken to report and remedy identity theft.

Credit Bureaus—Report Fraud

Bureau	Phone Number	Address	Mailing Address	Date Contacted	Contact Person	Comments	E-Mail Address
Equifax	1-800-525-6285						
Experian	1-888-397-3742						
TransUnion	1-800-680-7289						

Banks, Credit Card Issuers, and Other Creditors

Contact all your creditors ASAP. Contact each creditor whether or not your identity with that particular account has been compromised.

Creditor	Address and Phone Number	Date Contacted	Contact Person	Comments

Law Enforcement Authorities—Report Identity Theft

Agency Department	Phone Number	Date Contacted	Contact Person	E-Mail	Method of Communication	Date of Response	Comments
Federal Trade Commission	1-877-IDTHEFT						
Local Police Department							
Post Office							
State Attorney General							

To make certain that you do not become responsible for the debts incurred by the identity thief, you must provide proof that you didn't create the debt to each of the companies where accounts were opened or used in your name.

A working group composed of credit grantors, consumer advocates, and the Federal Trade Commission (FTC) developed this ID Theft Affidavit to help you report information to many companies using just one standard form. Use of this affidavit is optional for companies. Although many companies accept this affidavit, others require that you submit more or different forms. Before you send the affidavit, contact each company to find out whether they accept it.

You can use this affidavit where a new account was opened in your name. The information enables the companies to investigate the fraud and decide the outcome of your claim. (If someone made unauthorized charges to an existing account, call the company to find out what to do.)

This affidavit has two parts:

1) **ID Theft Affidavit** is where you report general information about yourself and the theft.

2) **Fraudulent Account Statement** is where you describe the fraudulent account(s) opened in your name. Use a separate Fraudulent Account Statement for each company you need to write to.

When you send the affidavit to the companies, attach copies (**NOT** originals) of any supporting documents (for example, drivers license, police report) you have. Before submitting your affidavit, review the disputed account(s) with family members or friends who may have information about the account(s) or access to them.

Complete this affidavit as soon as possible. Many creditors ask that you send it within two weeks of receiving it. Delaying could slow the investigation.

Be as accurate and complete as possible. You *may* choose not to provide some of the information requested. However, incorrect or incomplete information will slow the process of investigating your claim and absolving the debt. Please print clearly.

When you have finished completing the affidavit, mail a copy to each creditor, bank, or company that provided the thief with the unauthorized credit, goods, or services you describe. Attach to each affidavit a copy of the Fraudulent Account Statement with information only on accounts opened at the institution receiving the packet, as well as any other supporting documentation you are able to provide.

Send the appropriate documents to each company by certified mail, return receipt requested, so you can prove that it was received. The companies will review your claim and send you a written response telling you the outcome of their investigation. **Keep a copy of everything you submit for your records**.

If you cannot complete the affidavit, a legal guardian or someone with power of attorney may complete it for you. Except as noted, the information you provide will be used only by the company to process your affidavit, investigate the events you report, and help stop further fraud. If this affidavit is requested in a lawsuit, the company might have to provide it to the requesting party.

Completing this affidavit does not guarantee that the identity thief will be prosecuted or that the debt will be cleared.

DO NOT SEND AFFIDAVIT TO THE FTC OR ANY OTHER GOVERNMENT AGENCY.

If you haven't already done so, report the fraud to the following organizations:

1. Each of the three **national consumer reporting agencies.** Ask each agency to place a fraud alert on your credit report, and send you a copy of your credit file.

    When you have completed your affidavit packet, you may want to send them a copy to help them investigate the disputed accounts.

    Equifax Credit Information Services, Inc.
    (800) 525-6285/ TDD 1-800-255-0056 and ask the operator to call the Auto Disclosure Line at 1-800-685-1111 to obtain a copy of your report.
    P.O. Box 740241, Atlanta, GA 30374-0241
    www.equifax.com

    Experian Information Solutions, Inc.
    (888) 397-3742/ TDD (800) 972-0322
    P.O. Box 9530, Allen, TX 75013
    www.experian.com

    TransUnion
    (800) 680-7289/ TDD (877) 553-7803
    Fraud Victim Assistance Division
    P.O. Box 6790, Fullerton, CA 92634-6790
    www.transunion.com

2. **The fraud department at each creditor, bank, or utility/service** that provided the identity thief with unauthorized credit, goods, or services. This would be a good time to find out whether the company accepts this affidavit, and whether they require notarization or a copy of the police report.

3. Your local **police department**. Ask the officer to take a report and give you a copy of the report. Sending a copy of your police report to financial institutions can speed up the process of absolving you of wrongful debts or removing inaccurate information from your credit reports. If you can't get a copy, at least get the number of the report.

4. **The FTC,** which maintains the Identity Theft Data Clearinghouse, the federal government's centralized identity theft complaint database, and provides information to identity theft victims. You can visit **www.consumer.gov/idtheft** or call toll-free 1-877-ID-THEFT (1-877-438-4338).

    The FTC collects complaints from identity theft victims and shares their information with law enforcement nationwide. This information also may be shared with other government agencies, consumer reporting agencies, and companies where the fraud was perpetrated to help resolve identity theft related problems.

Name _____ Phone Number _____

Page 1

ID Theft Affidavit

Victim Information

(1) My full legal name
is_____
        (First)   (Middle)   (Last)   (Jr., Sr., III)

(2) (If different from above) When the events described in this affidavit took place, I was known as

_____
(First)   (Middle)   (Last)   (Jr., Sr., III)

(3) My date of birth is _____
                        (day/month/year)

(4) My Social Security number is_____

(5) My driver's license or identification card state and number
are_____

(6) My current address is

_____

City _____ State _____ Zip Code _____

(7) I have lived at this address since _____
                                        (month/year)

(8) (If different from above) When the events described in this affidavit took place, my address was

_____

City _____ State _____ Zip Code _____

(9) I lived at the address in Item 8 from _____ until _____
                                        (month/year)   (month/year)

(10) My daytime telephone number is (____)_____

My evening telephone number is (____)_____

DO NOT SEND AFFIDAVIT TO THE FTC OR ANY OTHER GOVERNMENT AGENCY

Name _____ *Phone Number* _____

Page 2

How the Fraud Occurred
Check all that apply for items 11—17:

(11) ❑ I did not authorize anyone to use my name or personal information to seek the money, credit, loans, goods or services described in this report.

(12) ❑ I did not receive any benefit, money, goods or services as a result of the events described in this report.

(13) ❑ My identification documents (for example, credit cards; birth certificate; driver's license; Social Security card; etc.) were ❑ stolen ❑ lost on or about

_____.
        (day/month/year)

(14) ❑ To the best of my knowledge and belief, the following person(s) used my information (for example, my name, address, date of birth, existing account numbers, Social Security number, mother's maiden name, etc.) or identification documents to get money, credit, loans, goods or services without my knowledge or authorization:

_____   _____
Name (if known)   Name (if known)

_____   _____
Address (if known)   Address (if known)

_____   _____
Phone number(s) (if known)   Phone number(s) (if known)

_____   _____
Additional information (if known)   Additional information (if known)

(15) ❑ I do NOT know who used my information or identification documents to get money, credit, loans, goods or services without my knowledge or authorization.

(16) ❑ Additional comments: (For example, description of the fraud, which documents or information were used or how the identity thief gained access to your information.)

_____   _____

(Attach additional pages as necessary.)

DO NOT SEND AFFIDAVIT TO THE FTC OR ANY OTHER GOVERNMENT AGENCY

Victim's Law Enforcement Actions

(17) (check one) I ❏ am ❏ am not willing to assist in the prosecution of the person(s) who committed this fraud.

(18) (check one) I ❏ am ❏ am not authorizing the release of this information to law enforcement for the purpose of assisting them in the investigation and prosecution of the person(s) who committed this fraud.

(19) (check all that apply) I ❏ have ❏ have not reported the events described in this affidavit to the police or other law enforcement agency. The police ❏ did ❏ did not write a report. *In the event you have contacted the police or other law enforcement agency, please complete the following:*

_____
(Agency #1) (Officer/Agency personnel taking report)

_____
(Date of report) (Report number, if any)

_____
(Phone number) (email address, if any)

_____
(Agency #2) (Officer/Agency personnel taking report)

_____
(Date of report) (Report number, if any)

_____
(Phone number) (email address, if any)

Documentation Checklist

Please indicate the supporting documentation you are able to provide to the companies you plan to notify. Attach copies (NOT originals) to the affidavit before sending it to the companies.

(20) ❏ A copy of a valid government-issued photo-identification card (for example, your driver's license, state-issued ID card or your passport). If you are under 16 and don't have a photo-ID, you may submit a copy of your birth certificate or a copy of your official school records showing your enrollment and place of residence.

DO NOT SEND AFFIDAVIT TO THE FTC OR ANY OTHER GOVERNMENT AGENCY

(21) ❐ Proof of residency during the time the disputed bill occurred, the loan was made or the other event took place (for example, a rental/lease agreement in your name, a copy of a utility bill or a copy of an insurance bill).

(22) ❐ A copy of the report you filed with the police or sheriff's department. If you are unable to obtain a report or report number from the police, please indicate that in Item 19. Some companies only need the report number, not a copy of the report. You may want to check with each company.

Signature

I declare under penalty of perjury that the information I have provided in this affidavit is true and correct to the best of my knowledge.

_____   _____
(signature)   (date signed)

Knowingly submitting false information on this form could subject you to criminal prosecution for perjury.

_____
(Notary)

[Check with each company. Creditors sometimes require notarization. If they do not, please have one witness (non-relative) sign below that you completed and signed this affidavit.]

Witness:

_____   _____
(signature)   (printed name)

_____   _____
(date)   (telephone number)

DO NOT SEND AFFIDAVIT TO THE FTC OR ANY OTHER GOVERNMENT AGENCY

Fraudulent Account Statement

Completing this Statement

____ Make as many copies of this page as you need. **Complete a separate page for each company you're notifying and only send it to that company.** Include a copy of your signed affidavit.

____ List only the account(s) you're disputing with the company receiving this form. **See the example below.**

____ If a collection agency sent you a statement, letter or notice about the fraudulent account, attach a copy of that document (**NOT** the original).

I declare (check all that apply):

____ As a result of the event(s) described in the ID Theft Affidavit, the following account(s) was/were opened at your company _____ in my name without my knowledge, permission or authorization using my personal information or identifying documents:

Creditor Name/Address (the company that opened the account or provided the goods or services)	Account Number	Type of unauthorized credit/goods/services provided by creditor (if known)	Date issued or opened (if known)	Amount/Value provided (the amount charged or the cost of the goods/services)
Example Example National Bank 22 Main Street Columbus, Ohio 22722	01234567-89	auto loan	01/05/2002	$25,000.00

DO NOT SEND AFFIDAVIT TO THE FTC OR ANY OTHER GOVERNMENT AGENCY

Name _____ *Phone number* _____
Page 6

During the time of the accounts described above, I had the following account open with your company:

Billing name

_____

Billing
address_____

Account number

_____

DO NOT SEND AFFIDAVIT TO THE FTC OR ANY OTHER GOVERNMENT AGENCY

INDEX

A

Abagnale, Frank, 2-3
Adjusted Balance credit card fee calculations, 94
AICCCA (Association of Independent Consumer Credit Counseling Agencies), 162, 186
America Online. *See* AOL
American Bankruptcy Institute, 147
American Express
    credit card account numbers, 88
    history of credit cards, 86-87
    reward programs, 99
AmeriDebt, 157-159
    legal problems, 159-161
annual percentage rate. *See* APR
Anti-Phishing Working Group, 10
AOL (America Online) and phishing
    companies most often imitated, 10
    origin of term, 7
    scam targeting AOL customers, 9-10
Aponte, Jose M., 60
APR (annual percentage rate), credit cards, 93, 110
    finance charge calculations, 94-95
    introductory rates, 93-94
        fine print, 110
Asian Pacific Economic Cooperation forum, 76
Association of Independent Consumer Credit Counseling Agencies (AICCCA), 162, 186
ATMs (Automatic Teller Machines)
    credit card cash advance surcharges, 89
    identity theft liability limitations, 19
    identity theft techniques
        prevention, 12, 21
        used by law enforcement, 21-22
        used by thieves, 20
    reporting card theft, 202
    PIN numbers, 97
automobiles
    loans, single inquiry by credit-reporting agencies, 141

personal information uses by identity thieves, 5
Average Daily Balance, credit card fee calculations, 94
Baldasare, Carol, 44

B

bank accounts
    identity theft prevention, 12
    personal information uses by identity thieves, 5
    reporting ATM card theft, form letters, 202
Bank of Rhode Island, 33
BankAmericard, 87
bankruptcies, 143
    effect on credit reports, 149
Beales, Howard, 154, 160
biometrics, 67-68
    earprinting, 69
    facial recognition, 72
    fingerprinting, 71-72
    iris scanning, 70
    privacy invasion, 69
    retina scanning, 70-71
    voice recognition, 69
birth certificates, 60
Bloomingdale, Alfred, 86
Bond, Derek, 53
Boyer, Amy Lynn, 58
brokerage accounts, uses of information by identity thieves, 5
Build-It-Fast, 150
Burch, Frank, 70
Bureau of Consumer Protection, 154
Byrd, Malcom, 53

C

Cambridge-Brighton conglomerate, 157-159
car thieves, 73
Carr, Helen, 10
Carson, Johnny, 45
Casey, Paul, 73

221

D

Dalton, Reginald, 34
Daugman, John, 70
debit cards, 97
    identity theft
        liability limitations, 19
        prevention techniques, 21
        techniques used by law
            enforcement, 21-22
        techniques used by thieves, 20
    PIN numbers, 97
debt management plans. *See* DMPs
DebtWorks-Ballenger conglomerate,
    AmeriDebt, 157-159
    legal problems, 159-161
Department of Homeland Security, Patriot
    Act use for identity theft, 4
Department of Justice, 124
DiCaprio, Leonardo, 2
Diners Club, 85-86
Dinh, Van, 29-31
direct mail marketing, 82
    privacy issues, FACT, 180
Direct Marketing Association services, 13
disability insurance, 108
Discover credit card, 88
divorces, credit ratings, 125-126
DMPs (debt management plans), 148
    See also credit repair companies
    bankruptcies, 149
    Cambridge-Brighton
        conglomerate, 157-159
    DebtWorks-Ballenger
        conglomerate, AmeriDebt,
        157-161
    fair share payments, 148
    National Credit Repair, 161
    self-imposed, 167-168
do-not-call registry scams, 18
Docusearch, Inc., 58, 65
Domenici, Pete (U.S. Senator), 61
Dorsey, Andrew, 46
driver's license, 73
    fingerprinting, 71
    Social Security numbers, 39-40
drug connections and identity theft, 6
dumpster diving, 6

E

e-mail addresses
    mimicing legitimate addresses, 8
    prevention techniques, 9
    scam targeting AOL customers,
        9-10
    SSL padlock icons, 9
    phishing (*See also* AOL and
        phishing)
        awareness of identity theft, 11
        Citibank, 7
        companies most often imitated,
            10
        PayPal, 7-8
        world-wide scope, 10
    spam, credit repair scams, 152-153
e-mail marketing, privacy issues, 82
E-Mail Preference Service, Direct Marketing
    Association, 13
earprinting, 67-69
eBay, imitated with phishing, 10
Electronic Funds Transfer Act, ATM/debit
    card liability, 97
    limitations, 19
electronically encrypted key cards, 60
employment application forms, 44
Equal Credit Opportunity Act, 119-120
    coverage, 121
        621-year-olds, 121-123
        reporting complaints, 123-124
Equal Employment Opportunity
    Commission, credit scores and hiring
    policies, 136
Equifax
    credit reports
        credit scores, 130
        obtaining personal copies, 130
    form letters
        dispute follow-ups, 197
        disputing information in reports,
            196
        extended fraud alerts, 203
        individuals reporting identity
            theft, 191
        requesting blocking of
            information, 204
        requesting removal of inquiries
            from reports, 195
        requesting truncation of Social
            Security numbers, 205

F

G

gambling fees, 115
Gilroy, Steven M., 43
Global Business Dialogue on Electronic
Commerce, 76
GMAC, 33
gold credit cards, 101
grace periods, 93
Gramm-Leach-Bliley Act, 79, 82-84
financial institutions, 82
opting in/opting out, 83, 198
pretexting, 82
versus state laws, 84
Greenspan, Alan, 127
Gruttadauria, Frank, 58

H

hand print recognition, 67
hand vein geometry, 67
handwriting analysis, 67
Hanks, Tom, 2
hard inquiries to credit-reporting
agencies, 141
Hill, Zachary Keith, 9
Hirsch, Stanley, 30
Huggins, P. Kenneth, 64
Hunt, Darryl, 53

I

IAFIS (Integrated Automated Fingerprint
Identification System), 68, 71
ID Theft Affidavit, 35-36, 210-217
Fraudulent Account Statement, 210,
218-219
identity theft
actions after theft, 34-37
new Social Security numbers,
40-41
awareness of theft, 11
by bank/financial institution employees, 18-19
by convicted prisioner, 17
electronically encrypted key cards,
60
ID Theft Affidavit, 210-217
Fraudulent Account Statement,
210, 218-219
insurance, 75-76
Patriot Act use, 4

prevention (*See* prevention of
identity theft)
red flag guidelines, 174
scope of problem, 2-5
stealing identity of criminals,
52-53
terrorism, 3-4
theif committing criminal acts,
53-54
actions after identity theft,
54-55
victims' follow-up techniques,
185-186
victims' responsibilities, 62-65
vulnerability of average individual,
76
Identity Theft Assistance Center, 75
Identity Theft Data Clearinghouse, 213
Identity Theft Passport Program (Virginia),
54
Identity Theft Program (FTC), 2
identity theft victims
contacting businesses, 174
requesting blocking of inaccurate
information, 174
income taxes and identity theft
during tax preparation, 55-56
file segregation, 150-152
using fraudulent forms, 56-57
insurance against identity theft, 75-76
insurance policies and FICO scores, 135
Integrated Automated Fingerprint
Identification System (IAFIS), 68, 71
International Biometric Group, 72
investments and identity theft, 58
iris scanning, 67, 70

J – K

joint marketing agreements, 81, 198
Jorge, Kathryn, 60
jury duty, 59

key cards, 60
keystroke-logging spyware programs,
30-31
Kindberg, Jack, 17
Korinke, Robert, 62
Kowalski, Robert, 52

L

M

N

O

P

364.163 WEI
Weisman, Steve.
50 ways to protect your
identity and your credit.

8/05

Credit Score

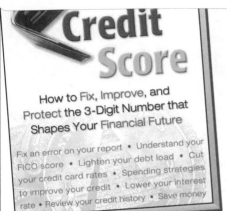

Credit Score
How to Fix, Improve, and Protect the 3-Digit Number that Shapes Your Financial Future

Fix an error on your report • Understand your FICO score • Lighten your debt load • Cut your credit card rates • Spending strategies to improve your credit • Lower your interest rate • Review your credit history • Save money

past five years, a simple three-digit number has e critical to your financial life: your credit score. It y dictates whether you get credit, it can dictate how much you'll pay for it. This book could save you tens of thousands of dollars in reduced credit costs, lower insurance rates...even better employment opportunities. Liz Pulliam Weston is one of the most-read columnists for *MSN Money* and author of the question-and-answer column "Money Talk," which appears in newspapers nationwide. She appears weekly on CNBC's *Power Lunch* and regularly on other television programs, including NBC's *Early Today*, to discuss credit and other personal finance issues.

ISBN 0131486039, © 2005, 192 pp., $17.95

Retirement Countdown

This is a step-by-step action guide to making sure readers have the money they need to live a long and comfortable retirement—going beyond the platitudes and abstractions found in so many retirement books. Retirement planning expert David Shapiro introduces a proven process for setting goals (Goal Oriented Financial Planning)—and achieving them in small, manageable steps.

"You cannot afford to be without this book on your shelf."
—Ben Stein, economist, lawyer, writer, TV personality and Honorary Chair of the National Retirement Planning Coalition

ISBN 0131096710, © 2004, 400 pp., $19.95

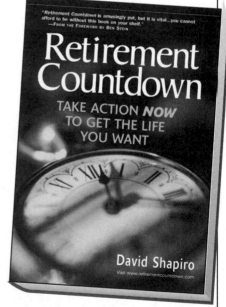

"*Retirement Countdown* is amusingly put, but it is vital...you cannot afford to be without this book on your shelf."
—FROM THE FOREWORD BY BEN STEIN

Retirement Countdown
TAKE ACTION *NOW* TO GET THE LIFE YOU WANT

David Shapiro
Visit www.retirementcountdown.com

HILLSBOROUGH PUBLIC LIBRARY
Hillsboro Municipal Complex
379 South Branch Rd.
Hillsborough, NJ 08844